BUCHAN WORDS AND WAYS

Alexander Fenton

BUCHAN WORDS
AND WAYS

With,
from Sandy.
Dec. 2006

Birlinn

First published in Great Britain 2005 by
Birlinn Ltd
West Newington House
10 Newington Road
Edinburgh
EH9 1QS
www.birlinn.co.uk

ISBN 1 84158 399 5

British Library Cataloguing-in-Publication Data
A catalogue record of this book is available on request from
the British Library

Typeset by Hewer Text Ltd, Edinburgh
Printed and bound by Antony Rowe, Chippenham

Contents

Foreword

I was reared in North-East Scotland, first in the parish of Drumblade, where I started school, and then in Auchterless. It was an entirely rural upbringing. A visit to Huntly, involving a walk of two or three miles to get there, was a matter of high excitement. Later, cycling broadened my horizons and took me to further off places. But though I was interested in the stone circles, 'Picts' houses', hill forts and great buildings of earlier times, my major fascination was with the way folk worked and spoke, and with the people themselves.

I used my mother's Box Brownie camera at first to record folk, though it had a bad habit of cutting off feet or heads. Later on, when I got to know David Murison, editor of the *Scottish National Dictionary*, I was asked by him to record words, and that led to noting details of what the words referred to. So an inborn interest began to be given shape.

The dialect I spoke was, and to a good extent still is, a rich one. I have never tried to discard it, and I use it as a natural means of communication when I can. To repay my debt to Auchterless and around, I have put it on paper in a volume of short stories, *Craiters*, that preserves and presents the speech of the area in the 1940–60 period.[1] This was in the days before many new folk with new voices had come to take over farms and shops, and bred children whose speech could not fail to modify – and in some degree also be modified by – their fellows at school. Unlike *Craiters*, which showed no mercy to its readers and had no

---

1. *Craiters – or twenty Buchan Tales*, East Linton, 1995

glossary, this present volume is a blend of English and the Buchan dialect, and there is a very full word list.

I am aware that what I am writing about now lies a world away, if not in time, then in the experience of the present generation. I am not sentimental about it. I am simply putting on record the everyday story of the people I lived and worked with. None of them ever seemed to think I was a 'deeve' with my questions and my notemaking, and they imparted their knowledge willingly and with pleasure.

The contents of this book were compiled for the monthly journal, the *Leopard*. I was first asked to write about Buchan words by Diane Morgan, then when the *Leopard* came under Charlie Allan, I broadened my remit from words to ways of doing. Much of the material is taken from my notebooks. It complements the study of *Wirds an' Wark* on a single Auchterless farm that I published in 1987,[2] and broadens out the picture. The two books are companion pieces, and complement each other.

In addition to my own notes, I have included the memories of older generations. My mother was brought up in the Keith area, and I regret not having got more information from her when I could. Mabel Smith, my French teacher at Turriff Secondary School (as it was then, though now it is an 'Academy'), can also take us well back into the nineteenth century, and some of the detail of what she told me or wrote down for me is unique. Willie Mathieson's notebook was also a rich source, and I greatly value the support I got from folk who wrote to me after reading my bits in the *Leopard*.

I am greatly indebted to my daughter, Lesley, who has done so much in the preparation of this volume.

---

2. *Wirds an' Wark 'e Seasons Roon, on an Aberdeenshire Farm*, Aberdeen 1987, various subsequent editions, now Mercat Press, Edinburgh

ONE

Some Buchan Words

The speech of the North-East is one of the best preserved in Scotland, still flexible enough to adapt to modern times. All the same, tools and equipment go out of use in house and steading and workshop. New ways of looking at the world come in, and words of earlier days, sayings and ways of speaking, inevitably fall by the wayside. We may regret this, but if we can keep a record of what is passing, we will still be able to sense the flavour and atmosphere of the days of our fathers and grandfathers.

The weather is something that causes great concern in a farming community. At a time of rapid changes from rain to wind to sun and back, a farmer was heard to say, 'It's nae wither, it's jist samples'. But few get as much insight (or as little) into the weather as the man who used to get up and look out each morning to see what the day was going to do. After a long evening session, he staggered out of bed half asleep and opened the press door by mistake. Back came the report to his wife: 'A mochy mornin' an' an aafa smell o' cheese'. 'Mochie' is used especially when the weather is heavy and oppressive. It is probably related to the English word 'muggy'. Dictionary folk are not quite sure of its origin, though they point to parallels in Scandinavian dialects, and even to the word 'muck', with the underlying sense of wet and decaying. But the farmer who used the word had too heavy a head to realise it was a puzzle for the experts.

*

Food has an eternal fascination, an' nae muckle winner for we widna gang far withoot it. But in the past folk were not as concerned as they are now with hygiene and pasteurisation and pre-packed edibles untouched by human hand. There are plenty of sayings to tell us so: 'Aabody ates a peck o' dirt afore they dee', i.e. don't worry if there is some dirt on your food. This goes back to 1721, when a version appeared in J. Kelly's *Complete Collection of Scottish Proverbs*. In the same vein is: 'There's nae motes in a moss', said if you dropped your piece when working at the peat-cutting.

If food was not very tasty, you might still be told to 'ate it up an' help awa wi't'. No North-Easter ever liked to see food wasted, so it is little wonder that the 400-year-old proverb, 'better belly rive nor gweed mait be connached', has not yet died out.

You can still hear of people 'rivin' at their mait', tearing at their food, in greed or great hunger, and so 'connachan' their stamachs', surely a great sin in these slimming days. Nobody knows exactly the source of the word 'connach', but it is a North-East word. Robert Fergusson, who wrote his *Scots Poems* in 1773, gave the first example of it, and it is true that he was an Edinburgh poet, bit de'il care, his faither cam fae Aiberdeen, an' he'd kent fine fit 'conn-ached' meant.

There was a tight-fisted farmer once, who kept a close eye on what his family ate, taking care there was no conspicuous consumption. 'Ca canny wi' the butter, wir ain fowk', he would tell them. Butter was for visitors, when not for sale in 'pun's' and 'pats'. And as my mother told me often enough, 'It's the hicht o' bad manners an' greed tae tak butter an' jam on a biscuit'. But for a growing boy, there's little comfort in being told such things. He doesn't want to hear that 'hunger's gweed kitchie', 'kitchie', meaning seasoning, being the same word as 'kitchen', nor that he was just going to get a 'dish o' tatties an' pint' for his supper –

i.e. as he ate the boiled potatoes, he could point at the hens in their 'riv' outside the window, and imagine sinking his teeth into better things.

Words can sometimes play funny tricks on themselves. Ever since I was at school, I've been noting examples. My father was a souter in Drumblade and then in Auchterless, and amongst the things he sold in his shoppie was 'blaik', black shoe polish, as you might think. But the stuff in the tin was so divorced from its colour, that you had to ask for 'black blaik' or 'broon blaik', and it wouldn't have surprised me to hear someone asking for 'fite blaik'. In fact boots and shoes were mostly black in earlier days and the range of colours of polish now is a sign of changed fashion. Ye cleaned yer beets wi' blaik, or ye blaikit 'em. And if you had a large family, and had to be thrifty, it was a case of 'blaik' one morning and spit the next.

Some words can die out in English and remain in the dialect. An example is 'pint'. This is the English 'point', which meant a length of cord or ribbon or leather, usually tipped with metal, for lacing up clothes. In our Scots dialects it came to have the specific sense of a shoe- or boot-lace. On April Feel's Day you would hear the cry, 'Hey, min, yer pints is lowse', and when you looked to see if one was undone you were mocked. And what would a visitor make of the boy who came into my father's shop and asked for 'a pair o' shee-pints', as if they were sold by sex?

Souters' shops were full of fairlies. The bench had a metal socket that held the iron 'fit', that could be changed according to the size of shoe or tackety beet that was being sorted. For home repairs, the 'fit' went into the end of the stout wooden 'deil' or devil that rested on the floor between your legs, or else into an iron 'saiddle' that straddled your two knees. If you were doing flat stitching, the leather could be gripped between the wooden jaws of a clamp, the 'claams', that also had an end resting on the floor.

Stitching was not done with a needle, but with a 'birse', the bristle of a wild boar. The 'birse' had a hard end with which the sewing was done. Nearly the whole length of the 'birse' was rolled on to the shoulder of the thread, then a small hole was made with an awl in the thread below where the 'birse' and shoulder were twisted together. The point of the 'birse' was taken round and through this hole, so that it was locked on and ready for serving its purpose in life, which was to guide the 'rositty eyn', the thread rolled together with resin between the palm of the souter's hand and his apron-covered knee, through the stitching holes. 'Birse' was expensive. In the 1950s, bristles cost about 35/- an ounce, or about a penny each. As a rule, they were used only once, but if someone took one off the thread for re-use, he would be accused of 'robbin the deid'. Since my father was a 'toonser', who learned his trade from an older brother, this must be an Aberdeen expression.

In Buchan you don't knit the leg of a stocking, instead you 'wyve yer shank'. It isn't clear why knitting should be called 'weaving', but there is no doubt that a lot of it was done. Aberdeen was at one time the centre of a great trade in knitted goods, many of which came from the countryside around.

If you were very eident, you could even knit as you walked about, with the aid of a 'wisker', 'wisk' or 'wusk'. This was a contraption for holding one of the needles. It was made of stalks of straw folded back on themselves, and bound around with twine, making a kind of conical rod or cone about 9 inches long. It was stuck into your apron band. One needle went into the thicker end, and off you could go, clicking busily, to fetch the cows to be milked. The word is related to 'wisk' – the kye wisk their tails tae haad 'e flees awa – and to Low German *wisker*, a duster. The ramifications of the kinship of words are always amazing, as are the changes of sense they are subject to over time and in different places.

Wool used to be bought in skeins called 'cuts' or 'half-cuts', a 'cut' being about 310 yards long, which had to be wound into balls. If you got your man to hold the wool stretched over his arms, you would either be 'stannin ower near', or 'tittin' (jerking), and he might let it slip off a hand and 'raivel', so that there had to be many an over and under of the 'ba' o' oo' before the job was done – a sure recipe for domestic tension. If you used a pair of chair backs, you only had yourself to argue with. There was combed 'fingerin' wool', a kind of 'wirset' or worsted, mostly used for women's articles, and uncombed 'wheelin', much coarser wool that did fine for men's socks and lang draaers.

My French teacher, when in her 90s, told me a lot about the old days. When she was young, there were no knitted jerseys or cardigans, but scarves were knitted, and left-over wool would make a pair of cuffs to cover your wrists in winter. Cuffs could be red, ribbed, or with a 'croshied' border. At this time you had to wear clothes after you had outgrown them, which explains the need for deep hems to let down, as well as the need for cuffs. If you wore a dress or coat that was too big, someone would say, 'That een's been made for yer growth'. A scarf was a 'gravat', which is a form of the English 'cravat', with a change of stress to the first syllable. Now scarves are usually of wool, but in earlier days aspiring folk might go in for fancier materials. An Aberdeen man ordered 10 ells of muslin in 1710 to make six gravats for himself and two hoods for his wife. He must have been 'a bittie licht abeen 'e gravat' to have been so extravagant!

'We'll hae a feast o' fat things', folk would say when a special tuck-in was on the way. Fat was what was wanted at one time, when hard outside work kept it from doing harm. They would scorn soup 'withoot an e'e in't', with no blobs of fat on top. 'Flannel broth' was soup made from milk and barley, cooked until the barley swelled enormously, making it fine and 'maamie', thick and smooth. The word is found as 'malm', mellow, in English dialects, originally from Old English *mealm,* meaning soft stone or chalky earth. But who would want to remember that when supping a plateful of 'fine maamie broth'? Sometimes this was made 'wi' the leg o' a dwinin' hennie', as the thriftier farmers' wives were said to do when the 'stame-mull' came to thresh the rucks in the cornyard, and all the neighbours gathered to help.

If there was something going on at a place, and a lot of people were about, you might say 'there wis a steer like a broth Sunday'. When you were lucky enough, in days gone by, to get a bit of mutton for making broth, it was surely a dish to look forward to.

It doesn't often happen that you find a word not in the *Scottish National Dictionary,* but now and again something new turns up. One example is 'stuffie', used for scrambled eggs in the Rora district. One wee lass got 'stuffie' from her grannie if an egg was cracked. When she went to gather the eggs, the lass made sure of the dish she loved by chipping an egg against the wall, saying, ''at 'll be anidder een for stuffie'. Of course, this is an example of what might be called a ghost-name. Grannie maybe said, 'this is fine stuffie', fine stuff, and the scrambled eggs then got the name in the wee girl's mind. We didn't have scrambled eggs in Auchterless, though. They were 'caddled-eggs', and that word is a version of the English 'caudle', a hot drink mixture.

When people speak of Standard English, you get the impression that it is something fixed and final. Maybe it is, as an abstract concept, but no language, if it is to be living, can ever be too standardised. Even the Buchan dialect is full of words that come from elsewhere. This by no means weakens it. Its flavour and identity grow out of the sum of its parts, and that should be so for the English language as a whole.

Sometimes the words come from away back in a forgotten time. We didn't always speak the Buchan dialect, which is a dialect of Scots, but also Gaelic, and even Pictish. Perhaps a lot of our words, and especially place-names, are Pictish, if we could identify them. It's a pity nobody really knows in any detail what the language was. But we can identify Gaelic words, at least.

If someone can't clear his feet, if he 'has nae ca-throwe', it might be said that 'he his nae farrach'. This is Gaelic *farrach*, force, energy, drive. It goes back to the early 1700s in the North-East. So far so good, but things get complicated if you look more closely. I heard 'farrach' from my French teacher, brought up in the Fraserburgh area. In the *Scottish National Dictionary* a second sense is also noted, a 'state of agitation'. This is what I have always known as 'feerich' – come on, noo, nae eese for haddin' sic a feerich. I looked up 'feerich' and what did I find? One sense is the one I know, but the other is the same as 'farrach', energy. In usage the words are certainly confused, but every phonologist knows that rules of language are regular, and though 'moon' becomes 'meen' and 'flourish' becomes 'fleerish' in Buchan, there is no way that 'farrach' can become 'feerich'.

We're not finished yet, though. 'Feerich' may be of uncertain origin, but there's another word, 'foorich', which means 'bustle, confusion', also. This is not only a North-East word. It goes back to the late 1700s in Lanarkshire, for example. The *Dictionary* notes that it is found in Gaelic-Scottish areas or contexts and compares yet another word, 'foorach'. This is a genuine North-Easter, a name for buttermilk or whipped cream or whey with buttermilk stirred in, which comes from Gaelic *fuarag*, 'a mixture of meal and water'.

So we have 'farrach', 'feerich', 'foorich', 'foorach', all with sounds that give a mental concept of mix-up, confusion and breathless bustle, but not all matching each other in terms of sound-changes that are regular in the Buchan dialect. I doot we hiv a richt feerich here, an' I hinna the farrach eynoo tae mak a richt glammach at sortin't aa oot.

Fit's 'at, glammach, did ye say? Yes, it's another Gaelic word, from *glam*, 'to lay hold of voraciously, to devour'. A 'glammach' can mean 'an eager grasp', or a 'mouthful'. Ye can maybe hae a gweed glammach o' foorach, if all this confusion of words from a distant time has left you with mental heartburn, an' a teem stamach.

Have you ever been 'in 'e hingles'? It can mean to be in a lazy mood, but also not very well even if not seriously ill: in fact, hanging betwixt and between.

Illness of any kind had home cures, many of them forgotten. They may have to come back into fashion if local hospitals are closed. If your finger was 'beel't' or 'had a beelin', a festering sore, your mother or granny, in her wisdom, would search the roadsides for 'a halin' (healing) leaf', a leaf of the greater plantain, and use it as a dressing.

Some illnesses were more in the way of imperfections, like being 'geck-neckit', having a slightly twisted neck. The word in older Scots means a gesture of derision, and the reference is to the slightly foolish look when you have a crick, permanent or otherwise, in your neck. It is thought that more folk used to be 'geck-neckit' in the past, because a mother would take a baby into the bed at night. Since she always clasped it in the same way, keeping it cosy between her and her man, its neck muscles could become affected, one side being more strained than the other.

'The pap o' the haase' was the uvula, in the back of the throat. If the 'pap' had fallen, and was causing pain, the cure was to take a teaspoonful of sugar and touch the tip, when it would immediately rise again.

There are many sayings about sickness or injury and attitudes to them, which were often unsympathetic, to say the least:

'Ye're aye half deid or ye be weel sick',

'Them that burns their airse has tae sit on the blister', are two examples. And if you were carried away with a 'kirkyairder' or a 'kirkyaird hoast' in the Howe of Auchterless 'you would finish up 'straein' yer beets in Moat's soo'. This is a euphemism only to be understood by a native of the parish, for the farm of Moat is next to the kirkyard. So putting insoles of straw into your 'tacketies', using straw from the sow in the cornyard there, simply meant that you were dead and buried. A hard kind of humour, indeed, but it comes straight out of the realities of earlier existence.

Not only people had their troubles. A common problem in the byre, for example, was that a 'caff', piece of chaff, would get into a beast's eye. You could try to get it out with the corner of a handkerchief. Failing that, you might grind a bit of glass into powder with a hammer, as finely as possible. This was blown into the beast's eye with a 'little tubie', to see if the watering would shift the 'caff'. Sugar could be tried for the same purpose. It wasn't easy to get out a 'caff', and if left there, a blue skin would grow over the eye, and it would water all the time. The beast's condition suffered, and the profits were lost. It's just as weel we dinna fatten fowk.

As I went around the North-East looking at older buildings about 50 years ago, I could still come across examples of a 'hingin' lum', a wooden chimney pinned against the kitchen gable. There was a time when most houses had them, but times change and many a home doesn't even have a fireplace now, but radiators or under-floor heating instead. 'Hingin' lum' is not only a Buchan word, however. It was used all over Scotland as long as the 'lum' type itself existed.

The fire under it could be at the level of the floor, as long as peat was the fuel, because peat doesn't need a draught under it as coal does. There was a bar of iron or wood across the inside of the 'lum', and this was the 'rantle-tree'. The word goes back to 1671 in older Scots, and its closest relative seems to be Norwegian dialectal *randa-tre*. This does not mean it has a Norse origin in the North-East. The term is widespread in Scotland, and will have come north as the Northumbrian forms of English crept up through the country, though it must have come into Northumbrian English from Norwegian sources.

The 'crook-an-'e links' hung from the 'rantle-tree', and held the pots and kettle 'abeen 'e lowin' eizels', above the burning embers. A common later alternative was the 'swey', which could be swung out and in on hinges.

If the loons made a 'bondie' outside, they would often end up 'birslin' tatties in 'e eizels'. The word simply meant 'ashes' in Old English, and the fact that our 'eizels' are hot might point to the custom of keeping the fires going all night, with the glow of life 'smoored' under the 'ess'.

A lot of Buchan kitchens had an 'ess-hole' in the floor, just in front of the fire. Dead ash was swept into it, and when the good wife was making tea, she 'sweeled' the inside of the teapot, or 'trackie-pot' as many called it, with boiling water, and 'teemed it intill 'e ess-hole'. 'Trackie' is from Dutch *trekken,* to pull, draw, make tea, not surprisingly since the Low Countries were a great source for the import of leaves. And if the earthenware teapot got broken, the fragments made fine 'lamies' for the bairns to play with. In this case, 'lame' is the Scottish equivalent of English 'loam', going back to about 1400 in Scotland in the sense of earthenware.

At baking time, the girdle was slung from the crook, and on it the oatcakes, called 'cyacks' or 'breid', were fired. The units that the round was cut into were 'korters', even though as often as not they were eighths. Besides the girdle there was the 'branner' with open ribs, for baking thick bere-meal bannocks. Another kind of 'branner' without a loop handle was laid across the fire to roast fish, sometimes. My grandfather, who served his apprenticeship as a smith at Kinmundy, made them. They were used in the towns as much as in the country, some for brandering fish, and simpler ones with two bars for holding pans.

Even in the days before motor cars and bicycles, there was a lot of movement around the country. Horses and gigs were the main means of locomotion, but a great deal of foot slogging went on. Some tinkies had cairties, but they still used their feet a great deal, and came to the door with their rigmaroles: 'Wash, bleach or bile, stumpet (stamped) throwe an' throwe, if it tynes ae colour it will get anither', was one way to persuade you to buy some oddments of material.

Though the sales pitch was enjoyed and remembered, the tinkies weren't really liked about the place, and the bolder bairns shouted after them:

'Tinkie, tinkie, tarry-bags,

Rotten sheen an' aal' rags.'

Even folk that looked a bit tink-like, with very untidy clothes, might hear some such shout as 'tinkie-tinkie tarry wallop'!

More respectable altogether were the 'quarterers', described by Walter Gregor in his *Notes on the Folk-Lore of the North-East of Scotland* in 1881 as a class of respectable beggars, who wandered round particular districts at regular intervals, being given quarters – hence the name – at certain houses. This name is found only in the North-East. To my knowledge, 'quarterers' survived till between the Wars. They came on foot and they went on foot, took a 'hairst' or a turn at the 'hyow', and slept in the straw in a stall in the byre.

The saying 'a lang road an' fyow hooses' meant a great deal in the old days. It was usual enough for a traveller on foot to stop at any wayside house and get food and a 'shak-doon' for the night. Quite often, spare bedding or even a low bed was kept below the box-bed for such purposes. My French teacher has told me that in the late 1800s her grandfather thought nothing of walking from Lintmill of Hythie, near Fraserburgh, into Aberdeen. He left in the 'sma' 'oors', which he called ''e cool o' 'e mornin'', and got back home late at night.

Fish-cadgers also went around on foot, but as the proverb goes, 'a cadger disna cry "stinkin' fish"'. In the days before public libraries, and even after, a regular, even if not frequent, visitor was the colporteur. Money was scarce for buying books from him, but his leaflets had pictures on them that pleased the young folk. He dressed well, something like a minister, with a black hat and black clothes, and good boots. And such folk were the news bearers of the countryside.

Household tasks were more numerous in the days before electricity and piped water. 'Frauchts' of water had to be carried from the 'wallie', that is two pailfuls, often with a shoulder yoke or a hoop to keep the pails from bumping into the bearer's legs. Other things could be carried too, like a 'fraucht o' peats'. Again, this was a double load, as much as an individual could carry. It is the same word as English 'freight', but came into older Scots around the year 1400 from Middle Dutch or Middle Low German *vracht*, 'transport, carriage by sea'.

To keep the fire going, wood as well as peat came in handy, and with a good axe you could soon 'hack enyeuch sticks on 'e hackstock tae haad ye gyaan'. At one time you could hack sticks in England too, but now the word is found in dialects only (English as well as Scots). It is an example of a word that, though widely known, has gone out of standard English usage. The 'hackstock' was a good piece of log that didn't split too easily. Though a lot of North-Easters used this name, I knew it as a 'hack block' in the Howe o' Pitglassie.

If you fell behind with the daily jobs, 'ye'd hae tae get a breezle on', but if 'ye hid nae ca-throwe', you might be 'aye in a hurry an'aye ahin'. If someone had an accident, and hurt a leg, for example, she might be 'aafa backset at nae bein' able tae get aboot', and wouldn't be able 'tae get aa her jobs behan''.

Folk didn't always show much sympathy to themselves or to others if they were hurt. A blacksmith about Huntly had a bad fall in the slippery 'greep' (gutter) in the byre. As he said later, 'I jist winner't if it wis worth risin'!' And a farmer who was bedridden, paralysed from the waist down, was visited by a neighbour. After the usual news about farmwork, weather and freens, the visitor asked, 'Can ye nee meeve yer legs ava?' 'Na', said the invalid. 'Fegs', said the other, 'I doot if they were mine, I'd gar them go'.

A long-gone kitchen chore was the equivalent of present-day dusting. In the days of peat fires, the peat dust was pervasive, and dusting didn't do much good. Instead, our grandmothers would wash chairs and tables every day with a soapy cloth, which was then wrung dry and used to rub them over. Years of such treatment gave the surfaces what art dealers would describe as a fine patina, further improved by the rubbing of 'doups' on chair bottoms at meal-times. 'Doup', by the way, seems to be of Low German origin. Visitors also helped, especially in the long evenings about the New Year, when tea-parties and dinner parties were in vogue, with a bit of playing at cards. For tea parties, the fish wife supplied 'yalla fish'. For dinner, this was the time of the 'eel-mairt', a 'stirk' or 'stot' fattened for slaughter to celebrate Yule – hence the phrase, 'as fat's an eel-mairt'. Aal' Eel was Christmas Day, Old Style, that is, 6 January, and that is when our forefathers cele-brated. And at this year's end, I'll leave ye aa tae think aboot sic

14

fairlies, an' tae haad hale Eel in yer ain wyes, and that, as the dictionary tells us, means 'to celebrate with abandon'.

'Pace-Sunday' was a time for hard-boiled eggs. In some places, youngsters would get an unusual treat, a whole boiled egg to themselves for breakfast. The standard thing was for the bairns just to get the 'tap' or at most a half. The man of the house, as always, was best off. He got any badly shaped or especially large egg. Any cracked ones were scrambled in a bowl on top of the kettle and each got a spoonful. At Easter, eggs were plentiful, thought mostly bartered for groceries. It was a grand day for the bairns too because they got to roll eggs. First they were hard boiled, and then they were painted with water colours, but there were old ways of colouring the pace eggs too. It was very common just to dye them in tea to make them a nice brown colour, and that's what my mother used to do. Or you could dye them yellow with the juice of the bonny yalla flooers o the fun busses, or red with beetroot. It was a great adventure to roll them on a clean grassy hillside until they knackit against a steen an e shell crackit, an a hard bilet egg aye tastes better in e open air.

Pace – under that name – has been with us for over 600 years. It is actually the same word as French *pâques*. It is a time of celebration for all Christian countries, and is associated with very many customs, though there is no doubt that these have long been dying out in Scotland. The custom of rolling eggs is one example. It was said in the 1930s that it was becoming rarer in Kincardineshire, even though there were fine slopes in some places, for example near Bervie, that were famous as 'pace braes'. As a matter of fact, the Monday after Easter or the Saturday before Easter were the pace egg days in some places, though now it is more or less confined to the Sunday. But especially the Episcopalians in the North-East stuck to Easter Sunday.

Seein I'm on aboot Easter, I micht as weel tell ye some mair. Sometimes the kirk session would hold a fast on Pace Sunday, and there was a feeling that you should be more charitable than usual then to less lucky people. In the 1840s, for example, poor folk in Caithness with no poultry of their own would go round their neighbours a day or two beforehand, getting what they called their pace eggs. Fither or no they dyed an rolled their eggs I dinna ken, though poor folk hardly have the energy for niceties. However, it gave them an egg or two to eat on the Sunday, and it seems to have been the custom too to bake pancakes on that day.

Pace Sunday was also a day for forecasting the weather. It was said in Banffshire in the 1880s that fitiver airt the win blew fae on Pace Sunday, that's faar it wid blaa fae for the followin quarter. An fit aboot the prophecy that ye get in Helen Beaton's book aboot Benachie?

> Fite Kirk o Rayne,
> Straucht stan's yer wa',
> But on a bonnie Pess Sunday
> Doon sall ye fa'.

Some o fit I've tell't ye comes fae ma note book, an some fae printed books. It wisna that I was tryin aafa hard tae learn mair aboot Easter customs at e time, an it's a fair bet that I could have found a lot more if I'd tried harder. The point is that life is changing very fast, and more and more traces of older ways are vanishing. All the same, I'm certain that a wee bit of digging would produce a lot of information.

I think we'll tak a danner intil e byre e day, takin care nae tae skyte in e greep. Most North-East byres had a greep at each side of the passage, at the back of the beasts' tails. The strang ran along the greep and out into the midden at the back of the byre, but often enough it got claggit up and so a regular part of muckin e byre wis swypin e greep wi e besom (that's a brush, ye ken, nae yer wife!), leavin e cassie steens black an clean an shiny, for the time being. The bree wis aye inclined tae gaither in a halla at e fit o e midden lachter – i.e. the site of the midden – an mony a story's tellt aboot mishanters there. One farmer coming home from the mart in a state of bliss styteret an fell half intae the peel, and happily fell asleep. When his wife found him, there was a collection of ducks around him, quacking over the conversation lozenges from the bag that had fallen half out of his pocket. Of course, they were meant as the peace offering for the wife.

Clean greeps and beasts fresh beddit wi strae oot o e barn, cairriet in on a fork, throwe e feeders' byre an ben till e coos, syne tuckit in a bittie tae mak athing snod, wis a fine sicht. An fin e beasts hiv been neepit an straed an watered, an they've sattled doon, an maist o em are lyin ere chaain eir cweed, e byre's jist a richt peacefae place.

Greep is one name, but there are many others in a byre. Each staa held two animals, and a wooden travis formed the sides of every staa. At head level on the wall in front of them was the heck that held the straw for eating (which didna stop them haein a chow at eir beddin), and below their noses was the troch for the neeps that had been sliced into a scull in the neep-hasher in the neep-shed, barrowed in, then carried up between the pair an cowpit in.

In some places, like Orkney and Caithness, the part of the stall where the beasts stand or lie is called the bizzie, though I never heard that word in the North-East. But one of the most interesting parts for names is the coo-binnin or sell that ye nott tae bin e kye in e staa. There were several kinds. The standard one consisted of an iron bar, maybe 20 inches long, fixed onto the trevis, or the top of it could be on the trevis and the bottom fixed in a hole bored in the stonework of the troch. Fixed to this bar, called the slider, by an iron loop, was an 18-inch length of chain. This was the trammle, according to a Delgaty man, but an Auchterless farmer had heard the name thrammle. It ended in a sweevle to allow plenty of movement, and the two pieces of chain that completed the binnin were fixed to the big loop of the sweevle. One had a loop end and the other a pin, and once you'd got the beast into the staa, you had to lean against it, reach below it for the binnin, get the open ends round its neck, then twist the loop into the ring, watchin nae tae snag yer finger if e coo gied a haive. Wi a wild crater, it wisna aye a chancy job. An older style, said to be for wilder beasts, was the bowsel, a solid iron loop round the cow's neck.

Aye, a fine place e byre.

The amount of work folk did with their own hands in the old days is something you can hardly credit nowadays. I winner foo mony o ye hiv iver tried e smiler? That's a big shoulder rake, used for example to gather hay left over from gathered bouts. There were two points on the shaft where a rope could be fixed, and the fact that the rope was as often as not wrapped around with sacking is a clear enough sign of how hard it was to pull. The old style had big wooden teeth, but the ones I knew had curved iron tines.If the grass stubble was too high or if you let the tines bite into the ground, the breet wid jist aboot stop ye deid, an ye began tae ken fit it wis like tae be a horse. It was used on smaller places long after the horse rake came in, and sometimes for odd jobs even if you did have a horse rake.

Another tool that I seldom saw in use but that was once common everywhere was the breem-dog. This was a heavy iron lever for hauling out broomstocks by the root, so it had to be big and powerful. It was smiddy-made, all of iron, with a handle about five feet long. At the foot were massive jaws the spittin image o a crocodile. One jaw was the end of the handle and the other was the end of the hinged head that had a cross-piece with a great block of wood bolted to it, to serve as a pillow for levering in softish ground. The broom was gripped as near the ground as you could get, and since the jaws were anything between seven inches and nearly a foot long (judging by examples I have seen), you could get hold of a fair-sized stem and do a lot of damage, swinging with your full weight on the end of the handle.

This jobbie could be done because you were wanting to clear some ground you wanted to break in, and that was common in the older days. But more recently the breem was pulled out to make stack foundations, tae mak a gweed foon tae yer ruckies. I've seen an Auchterless farmer's diary for 1923 that tells of going to the hill with the breem-dog to pull breem. But that's just another jobbie folk have forgotten, and even in the 1950s if you came upon a breem-dog in a neep shed or somewhere else on a farm, the wooden pillow would have been rotted away, as like as no, bit e tool wis still ere as a kinno testimonial till e hard wark o earlier days.

Iv coorse, e weemenfolk hid tae wirk jist as hard as men, and no doubt getting the butter to come in a plump churn – just to pick one example – could use as much energy as pooin breemstocks.

There was a time when livestock, especially sheep and calves, were tethered outside much more than in more recent days, and there were special stakes, called baikies, for this job. Some were well-made iron specimens, about a foot long, with a three-inch iron ring at the top end to hold the tether rope and swivel. Others were jist made o a handy bit o wid, as lang's it wis strong enyeuch. In more recent times, it was mostly calves that were tethered on the baikie, especially when they had been newly put out to the field and still had to learn about coming for their milk when the handle of the pail was rattled, tae spen em fae sookin e coo. Yowes aboot lambin time could be tethered too, sometimes wi a knocklesnorum, a kind of swivel that let two or three of them be tethered on the same baikie withoot gettin in a snorl.

The baikie must have been very common at one time. There are records of the 1790s about Peterhead that tell of milk cows tethered in the fields, and having their baikies moved a bit each day, in a kind of controlled grazing. It was said to be a very economical system, that didn't depend on enclosed fields. One farmer, a true economist, had a few sheep on longer tethers that followed the cows to eat up anything the cows had left, and what was more, he would make the horses pasture in the same fields, 'so that the tufts of grass produced by the dunging of one species of animals is eat up by those of another kind and nothing is lost'. So there's thrift for ye.

I remember once looking at a set of aerial potographs of North Ronaldsay in Orkney, and noticed numbers of rings that I couldn't understand. When I finally got there, I realised that these were the traces of cows grazing in circles round their tethers. Though the practice survived till recently in such places, it died out much earlier in most of the lowland areas.

When something like this has a long tradition behind it, sure as fate you'll find it in proverbs. The earliest reference to the word is in Fergusson's manuscript proverb collection of before 1598, 'better hand louse nor bund to ane ill baikie'. In Caithness there is the saying, 'tae poo the baikie', meaning to indulge a wee bittie, and in the Turra area I was able to find one or two examples fin I wis gaan aboot speerin. You might say to someone going off for the day, 'Ye've gotten yer baikie oot', or, according to Mrs Hendry of Delgaty, 'Ye've surely got yer baikie lowse e day'. In ither wirds, ye were aff on e ran-dan. It's aften e case at aal wirds are kept in proverbs an sayins fin they've disappeared fae iveryday eese, bit I'd be willin tae bet ye could still fin a neep-shed or twa aboot e northeast wi a baikie in e crap o e waa.

Another point that marks a long history behind this simple wee device is the origin of the name. There is a Gaelic word *bac*, meaning to hinder or restrain, and from this comes the name *bacan*, a tethering stake. The Gaelic origin is supported by the fact that when Fergusson's proverb collection was first printed in 1641, the form 'baikine' was used for 'baikie'. The name is found in Caithness too in the form 'backie', which is closer to the Gaelic, but otherwise it belongs to Moray, Aberdeen and Banff. More generally in lowland Scotland, it is used for the tethering stake in the byre stall, so you can see that the tethering stake points, if not to more conservative areas, at least to places faar fowk didna like tae waste onything, least o aa grazin.

TWO

From My Notebooks

I took a danner doon e road ae day tae Westerton o Glasslaw, aye on e lookoot for things o interest. They had a lot of interesting things about the place, not least a fine meal girnel. This was in 1959, and I hope it's still there. It was divided into three compartments, the left-hand half forming one unit, and the right-hand half being split in two. This meant you could have three different kinds of meal or flour in it, but the biggest space wid aye be for oatmeal. When I saw it, it was no longer kept full, but a sack of meal was dumped into it as required. This was a rectangular girnel, 8 feet long by 2 foot 7 inches deep by 2 foot 9 inches high, with a separate lid over each half.

When you had filled the meal kist (aye, that's anither name for't), the meal had to be compressed as firmly as possible, and this job was done by tramping with the bare feet. Mrs Brown, who lived there, told me she had been brought up near the Broch, and had to tramp meal there 'wi ma petticoats cleekit atween ma feet'. Then her mother came and stuck her finger in the meal to see if it was firm enough. The book by Helen Beaton, *At the Back o' Benachie* (1915), tells that the meal girnel stood in the garret and was able to hold enough meal for a year at a time if necessary, and that it was the herd laddie or one of the young members of the family that did the tramping.

Sometimes you could use the meal in the girnel for storing other kinds of foodstuffs. I've heard that mealy puddings were sometimes kept in the meal, which seems a sensible enough idea. 'Girnel' is an old word, first recorded in Scots in 1452, but I'm sure girnels were on the go long before that, for the storage of grain and meal has been a necessity for as long as people have been growing crops. It comes from a Latin word, *granarium*. So next time ye're trampin meal in e girnel, ye'll min on e pages o e Latin dictionary!

Fit ither fairlies did I see? Weel, there wis an aal baby's cot on rockers, that came from the neighbouring farm of Curriedown. But still (at that time) at 'Curries' was a piece of apparatus that went with the cot, by which it could be hung up on four springs, letting the baby rock on air. Maybe it wis a hame-made kinno idea, bit it wid fairly be worth patentin.

Douglas Broon the fairmer also showed me two threeple thraa-hyeuks, one of which he had made himself. These were ingenious devices for twisting three strands of cord, often binder twine, into a thicker rope. They were rectangular frames with three hooks each running through them, that could all be twined with one handle. One of them was shaped to be rested on a flat surface like the top of a barn weighing machine, with the winding part and handle overhanging the edge. The three strands being turned by the threeple thraahyeuk ran together onto a single hook that was being twined in the opposite direction, and sometimes there was a wooden tensioner with three curving grooves in the side that you pressed against the point where the strands were being combined, to make a good hard rope. Weel, it wis a gran jobbie for a rainie day.

I aye likit tae rake aboot ither fowk's places. It's jist winnerfae fit ye can learn. Eence fin I wis at hame fae Cambridge I bikit ower tae see a freen o mine, Bert Shepherd, at Over Tocher, Meikle Wartle.

We were baith students at e time, though he wis workin on a different subject. We hid a rake aboot the fairm and sure enyeuch, there wis a lot o fairlies.

In the corn laft there wis the fan, fanners or winnister, for cleanin e corn. Ye got them on maist fairms o ony size, though maybe nae on crafties. It was a contraption for fanning or winnowing corn, with a handle that turned a fan that drove a strong blast of air through the grain as it trickled down from the hopper. The caff blew out at the tail of the machine – it didna dee tae be stannin there fin e winnister wis wirkin – and the corn came out at the bottom, graded by riddles into firsts and seconds. It was hot, dusty work and I helpit at it aften enyeuch fin I wis a loon, fullin e backet o corn fae e great heap on e laft fleer an cowpin't intil e happer, or aan crankin e handle tae steer up the divel's win. I min anither name for broken bitties o strae wis cuffins.

There were some curiosities that were new to me up on the couples of the corn loft. They were rings of straw rope, a wee bit less than a foot in diameter. Bert explained that they were for binding the tops of wooden tripods used as kilns in the centres of hay or corn stacks, to let the air in and keep them dry. You laid the ring on the ground, and pushed the heads of two of the poles through from one side, with the ends splayed out. The single pole was then pushed in from the other side and the pole heads were next swung up, which locked the straw ring into position and made a fine firm binding. The rings were made of lengths of strae rape rolled into a ball, then the loose end was laid in a circle and the ball woven round and round this circle till a ring about three inches thick had been made, looking like a little tyre. Twine was not liked for the job because it was not elastic enough, and rye or barley straw was too brittle for making rapes, though it was perfectly good for thatching tattie pits and for any other jobs where good straight straw was needed.

We came upon two contraptions for tightening fencing wire. They were called taings. They were strongly made of iron, and each consisted of a pair of handles up to just over two feet long, coming together at a hinged head. Just beside the hinge, each handle was flattened and roughened internally, so that when the handles were gripped together, the palin weer could be gripped firmly at this point and levered round a straining post to make it taut before stapling it into position. The taings were novelties to me, and it is a fact that farmers have shown a lot of ingenuity in inventing devices for straining fencing wire, even though there's little to beat the rope pulleys, likely a labour savin tippie that cam fae e States. Another of the fencing tools there was made of an old rasp, about 10 inches long, with a curved and pointed end. You could hammer the point into the back of a staple that had been driven into a post, and then lever it out for re-use – waste not want not has aye been a gweed North-East rule. And just to make this simple tool multi-functional, there was a hole near the back end, big enough to take a loose end of fencing wire that could then be twisted round a taut strand.

The last thing I noticed at Over Tocher was a weed puller with two long wooden handles (or it would have had them if they'd been there) with a hinged head and two jaws that were just the thing for getting out dockens and thistles, and you didn't even need to bend.

Fin I wis a loon, rinnin aboot in Drumblade and then in Auchterless, I eest tae hear aa kins o sayins an turns o phrase.

They bade in ma heid, for they maan hae teen ma fancy, an onywye, I wis aye interestit in words and language. Nowadays some of them would be described as naive, primitive, even superstitious, but they were born of an older past and because of that they can reflect something of the ways of thinking, the humour and beliefs, of earlier generations.

Een o the maist fascinatin examples is riddles, an they maan fascinate e world o learnin as weel, for hale books his been written aboot em, analysin fit they mean in terms o community life, the relationships atween men an weemen, fither men used em mair than weemen, an sic-like, bit as far as I wis concerned, it wis e trickiness o em that held ma attention. An anither thing – as aften as no, ye wis expeckit tae ken e answer.

Here's an example: 'Fit gangs intill e watter fite and comes oot black?' Weel, it's jist 'a mullert's beet'. And so I always remembered that one when I visited Douglas Anderson at the Mill o Newmill in Auchterless and saw his white floury boots, which soon turned black if he walked through wet grass, and even more so when, as sometimes happened, it was time to clean out the long mill-lade that ran from above the Free Kirk. The water had to be diverted and when the lade was empty there was a whole world of life gasping in the muddy bottom, puddocks and fish and other creatures. The fish, iv coorse, geed e wye o aa ither fish, intill e fryin pan.

Another one that I could never explain exactly because the answer could have been almost anything, was: 'Fit gangs throwe e wid and throwe e wid an yet nivver touches't?' Ye min on't pairtly because e wirds clink egither, an e answer is jist 'a watch in a mannie's pooch'. It's hard to say how old this one might be, but it will not be older than the days when menfolk began to carry watches in their waistcoat pockets so that the times of yokins could be kept according to man-made divisions instead of by the height of the sun and the state of the daylight. There was a good North-East name for the old-fashioned watches, usually in a shiny metal case for protection. They were 'neeps', no doubt because they were fat and round, which was a good thing because they settled firmly into your oxter pooch and would not easily fall out. The first time the word 'neep' is mentioned for a watch goes back to Banffshire in 1866.

A riddle that has to do with a description of an object that you have to guess is: 'Hings heich, Cries sair, His a heid, Bit wints e hair'. This is just a bell in a kirk steeple, an it's a fine riddle tae min on fin ye hear e bell ringin oot across e parks, cheery or sad accordin till e occasion.

I happent tae mak a collection o proverbs an sayins in the 1950s. I got over 600 from the district, all from word of mouth sources. They were published in the journal, *Scottish Studies*. An old favourite is, 'Come a riddle, Come a riddle, Come a rot-ot-ot, A little wee man in a reed, reed coat, A staff in eez han, An a steen in eez throat, Gin ye tell ma ma riddle, I'll gie ye a groat'. Well, that's a cherry, but I think it must have been more of the eating kind than the wild, sour eens that grew on the trees, at maybe the blackbirds likit bit the loons didna. Another old standard that comes to mind is 'Iron jug, timmer heid, spits fire, spews lead'. It disnae tak a lot o thinkin tae ken that's a gun. Which reminds me of one of the more frightening experiences I had as a boy. I was with two other young lads at Upper Pitglassie and we came upon a gun at the back o a shed. One pointed it roughly in my direction, said 'it winna be loaded', and pulled the trigger. It was. I felt the wind of the shot as it blasted past my nose and into the creosoted timber work of the shed owerby. It's a winner I'm still here. Funnily enough, that was a cousin who had the same name as myself.

Besides riddles, there wis aa kins o sayings an bits o rhymes. I can think o a verse, not very polite: 'Fin I wis young an hertie, I hurlet in a cairtie, e cairtie brook an I fell oot, an skinnt aa ma airsie'. And there was a game the young folk played in Drumblade, where you were supposed to make a kind of nest out of a tuft or two of grass, and shout 'Kelpie, kelpie, herrie ma nestie', but for the life of me I can't remember the way it was played.

Once on the farm of Brownhill in Auchterless, I was speaking to the housekeeper, the late Mrs Brown. I happened to mention that I'd been lookin at hooses aboot e Cabrach, an that though I'd seen plenty o sweys there in e hingin lums, I'd seen nae rantle trees. 'That min's me on a tongue twister' she said, an richt enyeuch it's nae easy tae say: 'A rat ran up a rantle-tree wi a lump o raa reed liver in its mou'.

Douglas Anderson wis ma mither's cousin's man. His meal mill wis a great place tae visit, an ye aye got a gweed welcome fae Douglas, eez face lachin anaith e floory bonnet e aye wore. As aften as no, I wid be ower wi a wireless battery at nott chargin, doon in e bowels o e mull aside e pearl barley steens, an aye I min on fit I think o as e smell o electricity an acid as e bubbles rase in e battery. Ye hid tae watch nae tae get e acid on yer knees or claes as e battery hung on the hannlebars o yer byke, an you dirlin ower potholes in e road.

If e mull wis on, ye could aye get a lick o meal, comin warm an fragrant fae e steens, an at's anither yoam I winna forget in a hurry.

Douglas's father was a miller at Mill o Auchlossan, Lumphanan, but he died when Douglas was seven, and then his mother put a man in the mill. It was a two-storey mill with two pairs of stones, on the Finzean Estate. It was entirely renewed in 1914.

Douglas left at 14 to serve his time at the Mill of Kildrummy,

Mossat, by Alford. There was just him and the miller James Coutts, who 'sell't amon bicycles', and Douglas did most of the milling. This was in 1914–15. He served his time there for three years, getting 2/6 a week, staying in the house and being fed by Coutts's mother. No official arrangement was made for taking on Douglas. Coutts had simply come across to ask if he would come to him. So it was a kind of gentleman's agreement.

Douglas's first move was to the Mill o Fochel (he called it the 'Mull o Fuffle'), between Tarves and Old Meldrum, where the miller, Scott, had a reputation. Ae day Duthie o Clunie cam in. 'Did ye wey my cotter men's meal?' 'Aye'. 'Fit did ye wey it up till?' '12 stone in ilky bag'. But they were short by 2 stone a bag. The cotter men were entitled to 3 bows and a firlot a piece, sometimes more, a year, and this was their 'perquis'. There were 10 stones in a boll and a firlot was a quarter of a boll. Fae this ye can get an idea o the amount o meal that was used in a faimily ivery ear for porritch, brose, oatcakes and skirly. Douglas only stayed here two years.

In 1919 he moved to Mill o Fintry where Ogston was miller. 'Aye ca'd jist Ogston o Fintry. Jist bade a year. Wisna aafa teen wi e place'. There was sawmill work to do too and Douglas didn't like that. The mill had two pairs of stones.

So he went into Aberdeen to Scorgie & Co at 13 Rose Street. He was in charge of Hilldown Tree Mill at the Brig o Dee for two years, then was out of mill work for a while and worked on the roads.

In 1925 he spent a year at the Mill o Forgue, and then went to Crook's Mill o Keith as head miller, staying there for six years. This mill had four pairs of stones, i.e. two pairs for sheelin (removing the husks), one pair for grinding meal and another for grinding corn for feeding. The sheelers were of freestone covered with a replaceable emery surface, and the other stones were French burrs. They made a lot of pin-head oatmeal, which was sold to Colinton Mill in Edinburgh, where it was steamed and rolled into porridge oats and flakes. The oats for this meal only went through the sheelin stones, then went into a pin-head machine, made of two rollers with little grooves that cut against each other.

In 1933 Douglas started up on his own at Mill o Meadaple, Rothienorman. There was no house with the mill, but he just stayed in two rooms till, in the same year, he married Aggie and moved to a three-roomed thackit hoosie at Burnside o Rothie. When that was condemned, they moved into a council house in Rothie.

Finally, they moved to Mill of Newmill in Auchterless, where I got to know them. Douglas retired into Turriff in 1962 and died in July 1983. I got this information from him in his latter days.

Fa wid get tired o their mait? Brose three times a day might be a wee bittie monotonous, but there were a lot of other ways of preparing oatmeal and you might eat just as much in a day as if it was brose all the time.

For many, brose was the standard breakfast six times a week, with an egg for variety on Sunday. If you want a recipe, here it is: four heaped spoonfuls of meal and a teaspoonful of salt in the brose caap, boil the kettle hard and pour the water on, stirring with the handle of the spoon, which you clean by licking it. Cover the caap with cream from the bowl of milk that was standing by, and the brose is ready to be supped. The milk left in the bowl was drunk when the brose had been polished off, and that was you ready for the day.

Though porridge – which we called pottich – is often thought of as a breakfast dish, at home we only had it at supper time, and I think it was the same for a lot of folk. They were sometimes made with milk as well as with water. The liquid was boiled in a pan, and a handful of meal sprinkled in slowly, stirring all the time. Then you let it boil, stirring fairly often, till it had thickened enough, maybe in half an hour – a gey difference in time fae the makkin o brose. You would salt it to taste. In earlier days, porridge for the men's suppers was put on at the back o denner time and left to boil till supper time. This was a thrifty thing to do because it made the meal swell up very much, so that it went farther. Noo, there's a tippie for fowk tae min. When dished up in plates, raw meal was often sprinkled on top, and you supped it by taking a spoonful and dipping it in the bowl of milk on its wey tae yer moo.

At dinner time, an oatmeal dish could be knotty tams. I never liked it, nor boiled milk in any form, but there were times when it was that or want. The milk was boiled, then the meal was plumped in quickly, without stirring, and formed into lumps that were only partly cooked on the outsides.

Another dish was murly tuck, sometimes called snap an rattle. For this, you just heated the milk till it was loo warm, then you had to murl a quarter o breid – that is, oatcakes – into the milk, and then all you had to do was to snap it up. You could add a spoonful of sugar if you wanted. This could be used as a dinner dish instead of pudding, or sometimes it could be taken at supper time.

Just to finish my story, I knew one family near Turriff that never had meat for their Sunday dinner. They had milk broth instead, made with milk, barley, sugar, salt and no vegetables. Potatoes – not regarded as vegetables – were taken with the soup. Then came a pudding of some kind. This form of meatless dinner, of milk broth and then a steam pudding, was quite common at one time, but not necessarily on a Sunday. And it is no surprise that breid an cheese were eaten along with this. In fact oatcakes were commonly eaten along with milk puddings as well. So, with all of this, oatmeal was as much of a staple as tatties.

If you were interested in things, folk would be interested in telling you things. One day Jimmie Hunter at Brownhill in Auchterless came into the kitchen with the bottom part of a sowens sieve (sow – pronounced as in how), a rectangle of zinc, about 8 inches by 6 inches. The whole contraption originally had wooden sides, maybe about 4 inches deep. It was made to sit on top of a coggie or whatever vessel the sowens were being strained into. The interesting thing was that the wee holies in the zinc, which had been knocked out with a hammer and the point of a nail, were not just laid out mechanically but in such a way that the initials JH appeared, and the date 1840. JH was Jimmie Hunter's grandfather, and he must have made the sowens sieve himself when he was at Skelmanae, near Strichen. So there was a bit of pride taken in the making of such things, and to take the bother proved that the making of sowens for dinner or supper was common at the time, and it must have been a well-liked dish.

Some fowk'll be speirin, fit's sowens? You take the husks of oats, as left after milling, soak them in water for a week till the mixture turns sour, then strain them – and this is where you need the sieve. You get a slightly gooey liquid, which is then left for a whilie more, and gradually the heavier bits of it sink to the bottom. The liquid at the top, the swats, was not wasted but was used as a drink or to thin the sowens. These were boiled with salt and water and supped with a spoon.

There's a lot of lore about sowens. It wasn't just a North-East dish. You could get it throughout the country and into Ireland, and there was even a kind of trade in it, for in the early 1800s the people of Caithness were in the habit of making up half a year's stock at a time, letting it dry out in the form of a paste, and sending it to families in Edinburgh. There's nothing new about convenience foods. I suppose a proverb that goes back to at least 1721 sums up the fact that sowens could be badly made as well as well made, like any other of the staple cereal-based dishes of Scotland: 'Our sowins are ill sowr'd, ill sell'd [put through the sieve], ill salted, ill soden [boiled], thin, and few o' them' – a hunger food indeed. But they could be used at times of celebration also, sometimes made with butter for greater gastronomic effect. Christmas morning was welcomed in the North-East by drinking draughts of drinking sowens or knottin sowens, as they were sometimes called, and this was recorded for on 4 January 1869 William Gall of Atherb wrote in the notebook he used for a diary: 'Tomorrow will be our Sowin morning, as many people delights in running about from town to town [i.e. from farm to farm] and drinking sowins and getting fun, and making a noise'.

When I stayed in Bieldside for the four years I was at Aberdeen University, I got to know the ways of Aberdeen speech, not always the same as my own, and down they went in phonetics in my notebook as well. There was a particularly good line in abusive terms. Conversation with the speaker of 'Aberdeen' about a rather well-dressed lady might go like this:

'She's jist a trypie troliebugs.'

'Fit's at'?

'She's a strooshle buddie – a haipie kinno a craiter', or 'She's an aafa haip'.

The basic English translation would be 'stuck-up common trash', as was pointed out to me, which was slightly different from a 'proud stuck-up sort of person', as indicated by a question like 'Div ye see madamton up e stairs fyles?' And if a wifie was always spreading gossip, she'd be 'a big mooth'd claik'.

In the systematically derogatory fashion of Aberdeen speech, men got it was well as women. Of someone dressed up for an occasion, you might hear 'He's a gey ding'; if he was in the habit of dressing in such a way, then 'He's a dingy craiter'. On the distaff side, it might be 'She's a dingy chout', or 'Whot [not what] a ding she hiz aboot er'. This was the kind of levelling phrase used of someone who was a toff, or an imaginary toff.

It seemed to me as a chiel takkin notes that there was often a snide sort of quality about such town speech, whereas in a country context, drollery or humour had a more prominent part to play. If you were greedy, you could be 'Jist a Sannie [Sandy] siccar-soles'. If you were excessively greedy, you would be 'A wheety near-begyaan slype'. Of a cheeky little thing, the not necessarily unkind comment might be 'Man, she's an impident smatchet', and if someone, often a child, was being a nuisance, it would be a case of 'Siccan a fashious ted'. An ugly, hard-faced man was 'a grim goustie stock', and of someone who was hanging about the place doing nothing very obvious, it could be said 'At lad's smytlichin aboot', or you would ask 'Fit's e mollachin aboot here at?' Perhaps he might have been a scrounger, 'lookin for scraan'. If he was a rough devil-may-care character, he would be a 'roch haivless kinna chiel', or a 'gey allagrooze lookin lad', maybe a bit frightening if you first caught sight of him glaring in at the window; 'He jist gowlt in at me', so that someone would shout from the other room 'Fa's at skwallachin?', shouting. Aye, an ye micht be gey ill-peyed wi yersel if you got no sympathy.

Here's something from the back of my notebook. Twa fairmers wis passin Bennachie in e train. Een says, 'A gey hill at'. Back came the answer, 'Oh aye, it's a gey aal hillie at, I min on er fin a wis a loon'.

Then there was a superstition: 'if snaa comes on at a funeral, they'll gang tae hivven'.

There's a saying, not very flattering to the town concerned: 'I'm gaan aff o e face o e earth an doon tae Ellon'.

An finally, a counting-out rhyme:

> Eetle ottle, black bottle,
> Eetle ottle oot,
> Tak a nail an push im oot,
> For a dirty dishcloot,
> Ee are oot.

An for e noo, sae am I.

I aye likit tae be oot in the dark. Aifter a whilie ye can see an aafa lot, an if it's jist fair pick black ye can get ben e road on yer byke – mine niver hid lichts – be lookin up in e air an jist catchin aa ye wid ken o the even blacker uprights o e telephone poles. Whiles ye'd get a fleg, though. Eence I wis pedallin full tilt by Pitglassie, peerin up tae keep masel on e track, fin there cam a warm, furry kin o feelin alang ma neive steekit roon the hannlebar, an syne alang ma bare knee. Ma hert geed a richt lowp and I swivelled back an fore a bittie afore it daaned on's that it wisna the deil bit a calfie strayed fae e coort. A good job I didna hit it heid on!

It wisna aye dark at nicht, though. On 26 March 1959, I see a note in my diary: 'In the evening a tremendous show of Merry Dancers over nearly a third of the sky, stretching up in long white streamers to a point straight above, in the centre of the sky it seemed, where they flickered and leapt in great white banks, and through the planting to the East, a great yellowy-orange full moon between two black bars of cloud'. Ye min on things like at.

Syne I'd get back till e kitchen an intill e crack aboot things as usual. That same nicht I wis makkin roch draains o neep-clicks, wi widden handgrips, iron shanks an a twa-pronged hook at e heid. Ye didna need em in fine wither, bit fin it wis richt caal or frosty they were jist e thing tae knack intill e side o e neep an haal't oot o e frozen dreel. Ye used it in ae haan, an in yer ither ye held the tapner tae slice aff the shaas an e reets wi aa their wee toozles o dubby icicles. Ye could spik aboot e tailer as weel as e tapner, for it wis aa e same fither ye used it tae tap or tail e neeps. Ye could buy yer tapners fae e merchant, or ye could make em yersel oot o the eyn o a scythe blade, though they were maybe nae aye fully hivvy enyeuch for e job. Bit foo nae use a broken blade if ye hid een, an gie't a new lease o life?

Ye used e neep-click maist, though, for liftin tapped an tailed neeps intae the hungry moo o e iron hasher, wi a roon coonterbalance wecht at ae eyn, an e hannle at e ither. Ye vrocht it wi ae han, pickin up e swads or yallas een at a time wi e click in e ither han, pirkin em intill e box wi e iron blades in e middle, an wheekin doon e plunger tae sen e sappy slices scatterin intill e backet or e scull in anaith. Ye'd think e beasts in e byre could smell em.

Seein I'm on aboot caal wither, I micht mention that at the onset o winter ye hid tae get e feet o yer horse ready, tae haad em on skytin on e ice. Ilky smiddy hid its widden boxie fu o iron sharps, itherwise ken't as pikes or cogs, that were knockit intae the cog-holes on e sheen. If cog-holes hid to be made in new sheen, this wis caa'd 'frostin e sheen', so ye can unnerstan foo a cog-hole could be caa'd a frost hole as weel. Frostin let ye ken at winter wis comin on.

Auchterless is famous – though it never says much about it – for being the birthplace of James Leslie Mitchell, later known as Lewis Grassic Gibbon. His father came from Insch, and for a time rented a croft at Hillhead of Seggat, a place-name that afterwards became famous in his *Scots Quair*. He was born on 13 February 1901 at 'The Hillies', and went to Auchterless Primary School as I did myself. He likely went to the Kirk too, where a relation of mine, the Revd Alexander Gray, was Minister for nearly half a century. It's said that when Gray got the offer of the parish, he had a look at it, coming in over 'Derrie's Hill' (Darley), looking at the fair fields and fine farms of the Howe, and he said: 'Aye, there's plenty o siller, an plenty o sin. I'll tak it!' It's a place that's full of stories – and what place isn't in the North-East?

Hillhead of Seggat is close to Chapel of Seggat, where the farmers had been Wallaces since the 1760s. William Wallace succeeded his father Andrew in 1881, and about him three tales were told to me.

'Wallace wis an elder, ye see. So the meenister called a meetin o elders aifter the service, so the meenister says "Well, the crop is aal secure noo, fit aboot haadin the Thanksgivin Service?" "Aye", says Wallace, "bit fit like is't?" '

Another was that when Wallace had finished making his hay, he said to his men, 'Weel, we can be deein wi a shooer noo'. At the time the next farm Thomastown (Tammaston) still had a great bit to take in – but at least Wallace had no problems.

Wallace was well known as a great feeder of cattle. 'He pit a hale truck load tae London in e train fae Auchterless Station, tae the Christmas sales. So he'd a lot o drovers, an caain em doon tae the Station, ye see, an he met a man on e road wi a horse an cairt. They'd a job winnin by, an Wallace says "Fit's at craiter seekin on e road e day?" He thocht naebody sid be on e road fin he wis on't.'

There was once a man Jopp in Seggat (not the Chapel). 'He had an aafa racer o a shalt. He geed tae Aiberdeen in a gig kinna thing, he cam back fae Aiberdeen eence in an oor an five meenits. The shalt drappit doon deid fin they cam intae the close. He said if he'd kent at he widda deen't in an oor.'

A wee bittie nearer tae the Banffshire border, there is a farm of Floors (Fleers). A while back there was a man Robertson in it – 'a great drinker, jist near bade at Balgaveney (the local source of liquid supply). A comic kin o a lad, fin Gill (George Gill) cam up fae e Palace tae see a place, he said, There wis a lad cam up fae e Palace tae see e place e day, I dinna ken if he'd been e king or no'. Robertson wis a champion plooer in eez day.

'A deem at was a lang time at Seggat geed hame tae Fleers. She said at Robertson cam kickin in aboot ae nicht an fell in e midden. He jist sang:

> The dog in the midden he lay, he lay
> He lookit abeen im
> An saa the meen shinin,
> An cockit his tail an away, away.

Then there was Mid Pitglassie, in full Midtown of Pitglassie, usually just called 'Minton'. Sandy Wilson went into it, coming from Hatton Manor across Mains Hill. His son Bill was well known to me. It was said that e took prizes for horse, bit e hid a gweed man, Davidson, tae dee up e harness. Bill said he could fairly look aifter horse bit wis nae eese ahin em. He couldna dreel straacht.

The neeperin placie was North Pitglassie. 'Jimmie Allan wis there till 1921. He hid a dother Baabie Allan. There wis a fireplace on e fleer an a big hole for ais at wid o held a month's ais at a time. Fin they needit firewid, they wid pit in a hale post at a time and push't up aye as e eyn got brunt. He aye wore a gravat, they ca'd im "Mains o Gravats". He loot e place rin oot till funs an breem.'

Here's een aboot Towie. 'A Webster was there at ae time. He come upon e men throwin e wecht in e cornyard, an tellt e grieve at he wisna wirkin em hard enyeuch. "Man", said e grieve, "if they

werena able tae dee at they'd be nae eese tae me or you aither".' A
sang wis made up aboot it:

> Towie, Towie, in yonder glen,
> Happy are the maidens fair,
> Bit woe be to the men.

A lot of my stories came from Jmmy Hunter at Brownhill in
Auchterless, and here are a few more samples. He had a very vivid
way of bringing places to life with his memories of the people who
had lived there. One day I walked up by the Widdie to the now
vanished Croft of Curriedoon, meaning to photograph the fireplace, a gey hame-made affair with an arch at the top formed out of
segments of cartwheel rings. There was no sign of a mantelpiece,
and there didn't seem to have been a grate. Likely there had been
just a peat fire at the level of the floor. The house was a small two-
roomed affair, then used as a tool shed and reroofed with
corrugated iron. There were two south-facing windows, one at
each side of the door, about 2 feet 4 inches high by 1 foot 7 inches
wide – not exactly very big, and the only sources of light from
outside. The croft had become part of the farm of Curriedoon.

As I went up to it, I passed Jimmy Hunter pooin neeps in what
was called 'e Currie park', because it was next to that farm. He told
me that 'a man Gray' had been in the craftie. He had been grieve at
Upper Ordley in Auchterless, and when he retired he got this
croft, and made a kind of a living by coming round with a pony
and cart selling herrings from Macduff. This would have been
about 1910 or so, and he was an old man then. I doot he hidna
heen muckle saved up for eez aal age. The place had been empty
since the 1920s, but it still had the name of 'Aal Gray's Craft'. And
Gray himself had a fine nickname – 'Ah Hell'. Maybe that's what
he said if he didna get gweed sale for eez fish.

On the same trip I went and had a look at the stone circle that was marked on the map near to Curriedoon, with the biggest stone and one remaining flanker on the south side. I spoke about it to Jimmie, but he hadn't known of its existence, though it was hardly half a mile away. For him, the great interest was places and folk. As it happens, there are two other stone circles more or less visible from that one, on Mains Hill on the road across to the Kirktoon o Auchterless and on Fleers Hill. What with these three points of reference, the unfinished leaf-shaped arrowhead I once found when hyowin neeps in the Currie park, the flint core that arrowheads had been chipped from that I picked up when scything in the park abeen e road, the burial mound in Pitglassie Wid, the hut circle in Broonhill Wid, and the Bronze Age short cist in one of the other fields, there's an aafa lot o history aboot e place. It gies ye a queer feelin fin ye're hearing aboot aal mannies in smaa crafties aboot echty ear seen, tae think at ere's been fowk aboot for thoosans o ears afore at.

Sometimes I tak a tig at reddin up, and the other day when I was quarrying amongst some papers, I came across an old diary. It was for 1938, and on the front it said 'Buy the Best, Buy Latvian Butter, Eggs, Bacon & Lard'. It was an interesting period piece and it came from a grocer's shop in Aberdeen that was run at one time by an uncle of mine through marriage, James French. The map inside showed the way the produce came, from Riga by way of the Kiel Canal, and on to Leith, Newcastle, Hull and London. It would be good for the Latvian economy if they could start up the same trade, now that they have their independence again, though I doot wir ain producers wid hae a wird or twa tae say.

Aa this is by the by, though, for the main thing is that I used the diary in the late 1940s or early 1950s to keep a note of words and sayings that I heard from the folk around me in Auchterless and

Aberdeen. It's jist a mixter o aathing, bit I'll gie ye some samples. It
starts with two versions of a verse that I'm sure a lot o ye'll ken:

Here's Willie Waldie	There wis twa doggies
An here's Johnnie Sim.	An they gee'd tae the mull,
He's abeen him again	They took a lick oot o this wifie's pyock,
An he's abeen him.	An a lick oot o that wifie's pyock
A lick oot o this wifie's pock,	An they took a lerb oot o the dam.
A jab oot o that wifie's pock,	Syne they ran hame cryin
An a howp oot o the dam.	Lowpie for spang,
Lowpie for spang,	Lowpie for spang,
Lowpie for spang.	Lowpie for spang.
The cat's tae the kiln	
An the dog's tae the mill,	
Aa the roadie hame'	
Aa the roadie hame'	
Aa the roadie hame.	

When children were playing at hopscotch, as I was told then
'aboot 90 ear ago', they would sing:

> Come up an see ma garrettie,
> Come up an see it noo.
> Come up an see ma garrettie,
> It's aa furnished noo.
> A broken cup an saacer,
> A cheer withoot a leg,
> A humphy backit dresser,
> An an aal iron bed.

For girls' skipping games you might hear:

> Ma hert's in the Hielan's
> Ma shirt's in the pan,
> Ma wife's awa tae Glesca
> Wi anither man.

Most of the entries are in phonetics, since I was trying to get
the pronunciations exactly as I heard them, bit I'll spare ye the

technicalities. Here's just a selection of what I found interesting. It was David Murison fae the Broch, Editor of the *Scottish National Dictionary*, that started me off on this ploy:

The horse fair deniet [denied], the horse refused.

He's gotten e ploo streekit, he's got the plough started again.

E tool's aa up in a kerfuffle, the towel has become rumpled.

I could hear e dinnle o e wheels, I could hear the sound of the wheels.

E corn's jist in e deid-thraa, the corn isn't getting enough water and has stopped growing.

The hale minoarem o catties, the whole crowd of cats.

At tae's aafa wabblie, that tea is very weak.

He'd an aafa fang o a mowser, he had a large moustache.

There's one thing sure – if all the sooth folk who've come to the North-East study sic phrases, they'll fairly get roadit wi the dialect or lang!

'Hey ye feel, fit's e eese o takkin a picter o nithin worth?' I'd been busy in New Pitsligo, locally known as 'Cyaard Cyaak', where I'd been photographing thatched roofs with my ancient camera – this was in 1959, an I've gotten a bittie better a een noo. The trouble is there's hardly ony thackit reefs to photograph nowadays, and however good your camera, you'll never bring them back. And I wonder if the school bairns, who shouted at me as they came out of school, are any more polite nowadays, or if they realise any better that the old things are passing away and that there is something worth in making a record of the ways in which things change.

One of my pictures was at Hillside of Clochforbie (or Cloforbie, as they say), where I noticed a wooden peat shed made of backs with open spaces between. Leslie Youngson the jiner lived there, so it was easy enough to get plenty of backs and no problem tae big a sheddie o em. I've deen e same thing masel in ma time. His wife was there, and she told me that when you put up a stack of peats to see you through the winter, the outside ones were always ruined by the frost, but they kept fresh for years in the shed. It's a wonder that folk didn't have more sheds.

At Hill o Cook there was a teem craftie, and inside it a fine widden hingin lum and a box bed. The widden lum was a neat affair, built of planks and laths up to the height of the couples, with two 10-inch-deep wooden planks as cheeks that rested on two low stone binks at the bottom. There was no swey tae let ye swing pots oot fae abeen the fire, but instead a wooden rantle tree that ran across from the back wall to the edge of the loft floor. It was high enough up to be safe from the fire. Iron ones could be lower down. From this hung the crook and the links to support the pots and the kettle over the fire. There had been an iron grate between the stone binks, lying alongside when I saw it. It was a foot wide by a foot deep and stood on four 6-inch legs. The back and the bottom were of horizontal iron bars, and likely it had been smiddy made tae gie a wee modern touch tae the room. There was a 3½ inch deep mantelpiece at the front of the lum, a wee window on the left side, and a wall recess with a pair of wooden doors on the right. There wis aye the chance o fire wi lums like that, and when I looked closely I could see that the plank sides of the hingin lum were deeply charred. There must have been some bonny warm fires at a time.

Across the kitchen from the lum there was the box bed. How many folk now have had the pleasure of sleeping in a box bed, hearing the crackle of the fire as they were just doverin awa intae sleep? I was never so lucky, though I did sleep in a box bed in the attic roomie o a hoosie in Pitglaissie, and it was cosy enough without a fire.

A lad I met said the craftie had belonged to a man Bain or MacBain, who had moved into another croft over the hill and left this one standing.

Maybe aa this is naething worth, but it'll surely please somebody.

Few folk churn their own butter nowadays, and memories of the work caused by butter-making are fading. It wis an eident job, bit aa e same it aye brocht a bit o income till e hoose. My mother had a rotary churn she worked on the kitchen table, though there was an upright plump churn in the house, given to her by Wattie Black when he left his placie at the Hill o Hatton. It had the usual round, staved form of the North-East, and the plunger ended in a round disc of wood with six holes bored in it. One or two folk were still using them in the late 1950s. There was also one at Brownhill in Auchterless, but it was in the shape of an upright rectangle, and I doot it wisna as gweed as e roon eens, for the sharp corners inside were harder to clean. Ye wid niver get a square plump churn in the potestater o the plump churnin tradition.

When butter was to be made, whatever the type of wooden churn, it had to be plottit wi bilin watter afore the cream geed in. Temperature made a great difference to the churning time. At lang last, the milk was broken, and then the particles gaithert, and it was said that 'e butter's come'. If it looked as if it wasn't going to come, a cupful of boiling water could be added. The buttermilk was drained off, and often fed to the hens, though plenty o folk likit tae drink a cuppie o't.

The butter was washed in the churn with good cold water, this was drained off, and the butter got a second washing, this time with a handful of salt added to the water. It was then put into an earthenware milk basin that had also been plottit, and made up into rectangular 1lb pats, or small balls big enough to spread a slice of bread or a quarter of oatcakes. This job was done with a pair of wooden butter clappers. Different folk put different geometrical shapes onto the pats with the sharp front edge of the clappers – for example, at Brownhill, you could get criss-crossing lines making diamond shapes, or parallel lines with a cross in the middle, but at nearby Westerton it was just a set of parallel lines. This was handy if you were selling your butter to the travelling van, because the producer could be easily identified.

When I was in the farm kitchen one night, and the butter had been ill tae come, there was then some talk of bewitched stories. I'll jist gie ye een as I got it!

At Braefit on the road tae Turra they were bothert at ae time wi barrows rowin ower e close by emsels, an neeps fleein ower e reefs. At Templand a soon o bishopin (tamping down stones or earth with a heavy upright 'bishop', often made with an iron cart-wheel hub on the end of a shaft) could aften be heard as far awa as e brig ower e Ythan. James Hunter at Brownhill got the story from Geordie Reid, who was fee-ed there and was later fee-ed with his father at Carlincraig, but other folk knew the story too. And at Garrowood of Grange, Mrs Hunter's father, George Merson, had often heard a flail going. The story went that the man that had been in the place before had a great dislike for George getting it after him.

Hiv ye ivver heen a richt look at a corn laft? From the barn below, you go up a steep wooden stair, and into the loft, where the floor is swept clean for the corn from the mill that falls in a golden heap, dropping from the mouth of a well-worn wooden chute and leaving a slight haze of dust as it falls. The one I'm thinking about was a bittie dark, for there was only one window in the far gable, with six small panes, and the lower third was made of two hinged wooden flaps that shut with a sneck. Two skylights let in more daylight, if there was any, and along the plastered walls were four ventilation louvres that pivoted inwards and could be kept in position with a snib. So there were plenty of chances to keep the place cool if ye wis swytin at e fanners. And the other opening was a trapdoor in the floor, with an iron ring to lift it; in anaith wis e cairt shed, so that ye could lower full bags of corn to the carts waiting below, maybe not yet with a horse yoked in, but with the shafts held up on a restin pole, or fixed by a chain to the roof above, to keep the floor level.

There wis twa main bits o equipment. The first wis e fanners or winnister, that I spak aboot afore (page 24). This particular machine was made by Shearer of Turriff. It came to Brownhill about 1929, having been bought at the Curriedown roup.I doot gey hullocks o corn hid geen throwe er in er time!

The corn was measured in a bushel measure, filled to the top and smoothed off with a straik, a roller made of oak. It was not rolled, but 'scushled roon'. Both of these items came from Cyarlincraig.

Then another important piece of equipment came into play. This was the weighing machine. Its old name was the steilert (= steelyard), but up the Keith and Elgin way it was sometimes called the bismer. This one had a cast metal plate marked 'Wm Beaverly, Rothie'. It had been bought at a roup in the Rothienorman district in the 1870s-80s, by Jimmy Hunter's grandfather. This grand-father had a Hunter relation in Seggat, and he had been asked to get the weighing machine at the roup. The Hunters came up from Balthangie Mains in 1871, and farmed at Cyarlins for 48 years, after which Chalmers Hospital, Banff, let it to the Cowies of Tollo, who bought it later. Jimmy Hunter was born in 1887. The steilert was got before he was born, and went to Brownhill when they entered in 1922.

The corn was usually weighed in half quarter bags of 168 lbs or 4 bushels, whether for seed or for sale.

Jist lookin aroon, I saa a lot o fairlies. Slung over one of the couples was a scythe with a green-painted sned and a wire grass-hook linking sned and blade. It was unusual for a scythe to be here, rather than in the neep-shed where it was handier to get at, but the reason was clear – this was a worn one with no handgrips on the sned. Bit fairmers are canny fowk an they dinna throw things oot willinly.

On the floor and on the couples there was plenty of twine used for raipin rucks. I noticed a half-used ball of 'Robin Hood Binder Twine. . . . Treated against Insects Rot and Vermin', and surely as far as I was concerned it had a fine smell, even if it was death to wee beasties. There were also balls and lengths of used binder and baler twine, kept to be twisted on rainy days into raips, two or three strands together, for tying down the thack on the rucks. Twine rapes had by this time replaced the older sprot rapes, cut in the bog, but it was still the thraahyeuk that was used for twining them. As another innovation, there were several nets with 1-inch square meshes, used for holding down the thatch also and saving a lot of work.

Then there was a 3-foot-long han-barra or 'seck-lifter' for carrying full sacks of corn, a seck-barra with iron wheels and an iron mouth that could be thrust under a standing sack, and two wheelbarras, pending repairs. The corn loft was always a good place for odd sortin jobbies, because there was a bit of space available. Nearby was a green-painted barrel with a lid, empty but usually used as a store for hens' mait, beside sacks of corn, potatoes and hens' mait, and piles of empty sacks that could make fine warm hoosies for the wee mice, and next to them was the top of a Visichick brooder.

On the couples above was the body of a broadcast seed-sowing machine, in two halves so that it could be folded back when it was being transported. It was taken down in spring before sowing started, and put back afterwards. There were beside it some binder canvasses, two binder blades, and a 2-foot high wooden trestle on which the blades rested when they were being sharpened.

A round riddle had a zinc base perforated with $\frac{1}{16}$ inch diameter holes. This was a siftin riddle, for cleaning things like neep seed. Its wooden surround was $\frac{3}{16}$ inch deep, as was the rim of a blin siv, though this had a base of stretched calf skin. When corn was being sown by hand using a happer round the shoulders, blin sivs were used to carry the corn from the sacks to keep the happer full. They were carried on the head, for easy tipping into the happer. The two examples at the farm of Brownhill both came from Cyarlins across the hill.

Scythes were supplied by the local smith at Pitglassie Smiddy (the late Gideon Irvine, well known as Aal Gid or Brookie), fin ye nott new eens. The days of scything of crops are long gone – an maybe gweed reddance, ye'll be sayin – but still well within the memory of many. I've even scythed fields of corn on our own croft (we took ower e Smiddy Craft aifter Gid left it) when they were laid by wind and rain, and a fair tyaave it wis, but to see the bouts of cut corn stretching out behind you was very satisfying.

Two extra lads were usually got to help with the hairst. The usual ones were quarterers. They were Jimmy Gillan and John Reid, and they turned up regularly at busy seasons, especially hairst, for many years. A lot of stories were told about them.

Gillan turned up once at the door of the farm wheeling a pram that held all his worldly goods, an socht 'a drappie o milk till e bairn'. He wis a shortsome kinna lad tae hyow neeps wi, because of his stories, though he spilet imsel wi drink. He said he'd been in the South African War, an in e last War tee. Eence he'd teen up wi a deem aboot Banff an wis gaan along e pavement wi er, singin for pennies. They were singin 'Where is my wandering boy tonight?' when Gillan, steppin backlins at e time, geed heelster gowdie doon a coal-hole.

Reid – the farmer always spoke of them by their surname – wisna as gweed tempered, especially when the tobacco was going done. He just turned up by chance looking for a job, in Jimmy Hunter's father's time. He got a bed in the barn or the byre, and they tried him out on the shoulder-rake, the smiler, the next day. He tore on at an aafa lick, he wis a bittie roch kin, bit e fairly got through the work. He was said – or maybe he said it himself – tae be e champion pooer o neeps on Deeside. The late John Morrison of Feithhill (Feithies) had a story about Reid. He was coming for the hairst as usual, but started drinking about Turriff and had an argument with a soldier. It was said that he struck the soldier, and he never appeared after that. He ended his days in the common lodging house in Aberdeen.

When Jimmy Hunter's grandfather was at Cyarlincraig, there wis anither traivellin man, Jock McKay, kent as e Wid Laird. There must have been a lot of folk moving around the countryside in earlier times and right down to between the Wars. Onywye, it was said that the Wid Laird had come of wealthy folk, an aye drew money oot o e bank. He jist hid favourite placies faar e widda putten in a nicht. He comes oot o e barn ae mornin as Jimmy Hunter's father widda been aboot e close. 'Aye', says he, 'Jock McKay, ye're here.' 'Aye', says Jock. 'I jist craalet doon at e side o e wechts [weighing machine].' He wis a great eater an aboot e wik-eyn e'd get a great dish o broth an tatties in a thing like a milk dish. 'The Book's leein', said Jock, 'if ye're nae rewardit for yer kindness.'

There's nae doot there's a lot o lore aboot e countryside, and stories like this help a lot to preserve memories of days gone past, as well as the atmosphere of the time. A lot geed on at younger fowk noo ken naething aboot.

Things dinna aye jist work oot as they should. I've tellt ye aboot e fanners in e corn laft at Broonhill, but there were bits of an old one there too. It had never been a success. It had been made by John Hunter, Millwright, Wartle, a cousin of James Hunter at the farm, for George Merson at North Pitglassie, but it turned out to be too stiff to drive. So for some reason it landed in the loft at Broonhill. The hopper sat on the couples, and part of one side was used as a sledge on snaavy days. Country folk are aye gweed at recycling things.

Just to the left of the corn loft door was the cast-iron corn bruiser, green-painted, on four legs and with a cone-shaped hopper that was painted red inside. There was a wheel to regulate the pressure so that the bruise for the horses' feed could be made thicker or thinner, nae doot tae suit aa kin's o equine palates, and the maker was Harrison, McGregor & Co., Leigh, England. It was a No 5 model. When the Hunters moved into the place, it was taken over on valuation.

The bruiser was driven directly by the engine, by way of a belt from below. The bruise was allowed to heap up in the corner of the loft and was taken to the bruise box in the stable as required, to be dished out to the horses in the wooden lippie, a square container that served as the feed measure. Some of the bruise might be bagged.

The big wheel had a closely-grooved surface, though this wasn't original. It was due to a refacing process done by Shearer of Turriff in the 1960s.

For carrying corn to the fanners or cowpin it intil bags there was a wooden backet with a sheet-metal bottom. This one was made by a mannie in Turriff, by the name o Jimmy Ogg, at worked a bit wi Bruce e jiner. Ogg wasn't a joiner to trade, but was a retired grieve. The fine thing about it was the way the constant friction from handling the corn had polished the wood and raised the grain into very attractive relief.

In the barn below stood a bonnie widden mullie made by William Alexander, Ribrae, Turriff, N.B. [North Britain], Millwright and Engineer. This information was on an oval wooden plaque bolted onto the side of the mill, and made a good piece of folk art, for it was in red lettering outlined in black, on a gold background. This was a three shaker mill, an fine I min trampin strae at the strae eyn o e barn on thrashin days, a richt styooie job, needing all your time to keep up as the straw came off the roaring mill. Nose, eyes and throat got full of black dust but later on a good dose of fresh air outside cleared it fine.

There wasn't much stored in the strae eyn because it had to be kept clear for regular replacements, but the tummlin tam was stored here, a wooden, horse-drawn hay-gatherer, with a 10-foot beam, two bowed handles and six long wooden tines, made by Alexr. Jack & Sons, Maybole.

Though ye could see that things were changin, as ye lookit at bits o equipment that were gaan oot o eese, ye could see em still in a livin settin, an that's maybe mair than ony museum can iver dee.

At the back of the barn at Brownhill was the engine house, containing the sturdy paraffin engine made by Allan Brothers. The brass plate on the cylinder read 'Allan Brothers, "Allan", Makers,

Oil Engine, Aberdeen'. It wis a muckle breet o a thing wi twa fly-wheels, an man it wis jist aafa fine fin it wis wirkin, wi e governors birlin sae faist ye couldna see em, an e fly-wheels gaan roon as gin ey'd nivver be able tae stop again. A wooden shelf nailed to the couples in a back corner held a can of oil, a file with a turned wooden handle, a tin of grease and a cardboard notice:

> The Allan Oil Engine. Caution. Never work the engine without water in the cylinder jacket. Always keep the cylinder tank full. If at any time the cylinder gets much hotter than the tank, then the circulation must be defective, and the pipes should be cleaned. If the engine is exposed to frost when not working, the water in the jacket is in danger of being frozen, and consequently breakage may ensue. In frosty weather, particular attention must be paid to close the circulating cock at tank, open the small cock on the bottom water pipe, and run the water off from the tanks, until the top water pipe and the cylinder jacket is empty.

No doubt careful attention was paid to these instructions, for the ingine's aye there, an could be smairtly pit intae wirkin order.

The 'Allan' drove the mullie for the weekly thrash. But besides this, the traivellin mull wid come alang, usually in e simmer, aboot June. Sometimes it was Wilson o Turra, sometimes Easton o Pitcaple (who had a Garvie of Aberdeen mill), and sometimes Christie o Rothie Vale (between Rothienorman and Fyvie), in the days of the tractor-driven ones. Earlier on it wis e stame mull – Ducat o Arnhead. I heard a story about him. Ducat wis there ae nicht, it cam on an aafa thunnerstorm. They hid a larry an jist beddit up for e nicht. Aye ere cam on anither flash an is lichtit up a dose o chuckens reestit in e boortree. Ducat couldna unnerstan fit is wis an hid tae rise tae gang an see. I just hope he got some satisfaction! Fin Ducat roupit oot o Arnhead, e kitchen dresser wis bocht for Broonhill.

As a matter o interest, the meal girnel in the chaamer at Brownhill cam frae e same roup. Like a lot of other things on the farm, furniture as well as tools, there was a good deal of recycling of items through farm sales. It was seldom that spleet new things were bought, and most of what was acquired at roups came from within a 10- or 12-mile radius, jist fit wis handy, and the feeling of having got a bargain was strong. But what was bought then was bought for use. Nowadays, though, there is brisk enough bidding at roups for older-fashioned things, often of the horse era, but it is only to keep them as ornaments, or put them into a museum, and though it is maybe the only way to preserve them, still an on it's maybe a peety tae see things that played a main role in iveryday life an wark turnin intae dealers' items or decorations. That's what the 'experts' call musealisation!

I'd like tae tell ye aboot honey ale as a hairst drink. When corn was being cut or led, it was the job of the women of the house to carry the piece out to the field, tea with sugar and milk – in the older days you were never asked if you took milk and sugar, you just got it – scones and bannocks wi butter, an fit wis a special treat, honey ale. Honey ale was made quite often at Brownhill and it made a fine drink that tickled yer moo an jist aboot geed roon yer hert like a hairy worm. The wye ye made it wis tae pit comb honey intill a muslin bag an hing it up tae dreep ower a basin. Syne ye steepit fit wis left in e baggie. Ye'd get a slice o loaf on e eyn o a fork an toast it in front o e bars o e grate, an clairt some yeast on e tap. The liquid strained aff aifter steepin e leavins o e comb wis put intill a pot, an e breid wis floatit on e tap. Syne you covered the pot with a cloth and left it for three days to a week to work. Aifter at, ye jist bottlet it an left it in e milkhoose for a day or twa, an it wis ready for drinkin. I suppose it was just a kind of mead, an I'm sure it tastit a lot better than the professional stuff that you can get from Lindisfarne nowadays. At least you got mair o a fine yoam o honey intae yer moo, though it maybe wisna jist aa that strong. All the same, it was pretty volatile stuff and liable to blow the cork, or even burst the bottle if you'd jammed the cork in too hard. Half the bottle was often lost in the park because it frothed up too fast just with being carried out.

Nowadays the type of fork usually used about the place is a general-purpose one with fairly wide and long and slightly curved prongs. But for hairst work, a more specialised one with much shorter, closer prongs was jist e very dab. This was the shafe-fork, fine and handy for forkin at e ruck when it was necessary to place the sheaves precisely at the hand of the man that was biggin, makkin sure at e shear o e shafe lay e richt wye up.

I fairly likit e shafe fork, since forking was one of my regular jobs, but not every job was so pleasant. I nivver likit haein tae tramp e strae in e strae-eyn o e barn, as it cam aff e shakkers o e mull. It wis ower full o styoo. But it had to be well tramped down to pack in as much as possible, layer upon layer. However, there was an older style of handling the straw. This was to make it into winnlins, a system used especially at water-driven mills that were a bit away from the rest of the houses, and where the barn space was small. The straw as it was threshed was made into bunches that would fit into the crook of your arm. The thinner ends were turned back and twined round to make a compact mass that would not spill out straw as you carried it home into the close.

This is a very old system of handling straw. A windle or winnlin was what in English is called a bottle of straw. It could mean an average-sized bunch, but it could also be a specific measure, reckoned at a fortieth part of a kemple, and weighing about 6 to 9 pounds avoirdupois. Before the days o the mullie, it wis a regular job, makkin winnlins, and at e same time it wis e wye ye wirkit oot e size o yer strae – or hey – crap.

Thinkin aboot e Olympics, maybe we hid jist aboot as gweed wecht lifters on e fairms in e days afore liftin technology. I min on loadin a tractor bogey wi bags o manure aa be masel eence, an I wis aye ready tae try ma strinth – an nae doot at's e wye I've heen stiff shooders ivver since! Young fowk's nae aye jist as wise as ey sid be.

We'll hae a look at e neep-shed at Broonhill e day. It's aye interestin tae quarry in ony place aboot a fairm. Ye can learn an aafa lot aboot its wyes o wirkin an its aaler history jist be lookin at e tools an equipment.

Ah weel, e neep-shed hid a big reed-paintit double sliding door, big enyeuch tae back in a cairt, an a second up-an-doon slidin door leadin intill e byre. It wis ceiled, wi e hey-laft abeen, an e fleer wis cobbled. Licht cam throwe e open doors an fae a wee skylicht at e back, that ye could open wi a rope an pulley.

The stock of turnips lay in the middle of the floor where they had been coupit oot o e cairt, and all around on the floor and stuck into the wood panelling of the walls were various items. There was a two-drill scarifier made by George Sellar & Son Ltd, Agricultural Engineers, Huntly & Alloa. This happened to belong to Davy Minto at Mid Pitglassie and was waiting to be returned. A two-drill neep-shaaver, with two cast-iron concave rollers and a wooden roller behind the spoots that ran from the seed boxes, had been made by Mennie, the smith at Fortrie

Smiddy. It had a pair of handles within which the mannie walked, and a chain and hooks for fixing the single horse in front. There was an iron-framed happer for sowing seed, manure, etc., with canvas straps for fixing it round the shoulders. Happers were bocht at e saiddlers, if ye didna pick em up at a roup.

The Davie Broon tractor was garaged here, and there were green-painted scythes, and a wire backet, bought at Anderson's roup. He was the smith at Pitglassie Smiddy before Gideon Irvine. Syne ere wis odds an eyns – twa sculls for neeps, twa graips, an iron-heidit rake that came from Gideon's roup, and that was mostly used for reddin up in e cornyard, a tramp-pick for makkin holes in e grun an for leverin oot posts, with the name Watt stamped on the foot rest. He was thought to be a smith that had once worked at Fortrie Smiddy. The tramp pick came from Tollo Croft, where Jimmy Hunter's father had stayed when he was working at Cyarlincraig.

That's maybe enyeuch aboot e things in e neep shed. Tae feenish aff wi, I'll tell ye aboot a mannie Gray fae Curriedoon Craft. He was grieve at Ordley, an like a lot o Buchan chiels, he sometimes hid a weird sense o humour. There wis is time e tellt e men tae gang an fur up e tatties, an said till em jist tae begin at e side neesht e tatties. Maybe ye hiv tae claa yer heid tae see e joke.

He was a little man, but swack. There wis eence said tae be a challenge race on fit roon e boons o Ordley, an Gray won. He was said to have done it in twenty minutes, but Jimmy Hunter, who told me the story, had his doubts.

After he retired from farm work, he took up selling herring, but he had stopped this by 1922. Ae day at denner time, they startit tae

spik aboot plooin an harness cleanin an e wird turned tae somebody at hid a name for't. Gray says ah weel e could clean harness
some, bit e wisna naething o a plooer.

Some folk might think that to keep a record of such things is a
lot of nonsense, whether the stuff in the neep shed or the stories
about folk, but the fact is that this is as close as you can get now to
the atmosphere of times that have nearly passed out of memory.
And I confess that I am heartily glad now that I had the interest
even as a boy to catch and keep as much as I could. Fowk are aye
gabbin on aboot identity nooadays; weel, ye can get some o't here.

This time I'm gaan tae tell ye aboot some o e lads at vrocht at
Broonhill. When the Hunters first came here, a man called Willie
Laing was the bailie. He was nicknamed Groatie Laing, because
'he spak a lot aboot a groat'. Ony kinna oddity could gie ye a
nickname. He had two kists, een for eez siller and een for eez claes.
He stayed in the chaamer and used a gas tin for his water – this was
the time when acetylene lamps were on the go on bykes – but a
man Simpson at the next farm, Uppermill, when the Michies were
there (an ill-trickit kinna chiel), persuaded a loon to bore holes in e
fit o't. Iv coorse, it didna haad in ahin at. Simpson was a good
ploughman and made a bonny job at Uppermill with three horses
in a double-furrow plough.

After Laing had been there for the winter half 'ear, Willie
Beddie cam hame at the Mey term. Jimmie Hunter himself wasn't
too well during the first summer in the early 1900s at Brownhill, so
a man called Geordie Sim was fee-ed to work the horse. He was 'a
hivvy kinna lad, puffin an blaain a bittie'. Once when the binder
was in action, 'e forks at caaed aff e shaves, they were gaan roon an
roon an e craaled in aneth er tae see fit wis wrang. "'Ere's nae
muckle", says he, "at I dinna ken aboot a binder".' But he couldn't

make out what was wrong so Jimmie Hunter had a look and saw at once that the check spring was broken.

It disna dee tae blaa.

Rucks have nearly disappeared from all knowledge by the younger folk, yet at one time they were amongst the main features of the autumn and winter farm-steadings. Now the cornyards lie neglected or are used for something else. The impact of the combine-harvester has been truly amazing, and in a very short time. Earlier on, as you travelled the country, you could see how the shapes and sizes of the rucks were adapted to suit the different areas and the different scales of farming. In the crofting districts of the North and West of Scotland they were quite small, say 5 feet round by about 7 feet high. As a rule they were built in the shape of cones that started to narrow gey near fae the foon, but in some districts they had shanks like upright cylinders, whether they were bigger or smaller, with a kind of conical hat on top. By the time you got to the South East of Scotland, the rucks were more like 15 feet round and 18 feet high. In fact, they were so big that a female farm-worker, called a striddler, had to stand on the stack as it wis bein biggit, to take the sheaves from the forker below and pass them to the man who was biggin the ruck. Bit ye didna get that in e North-East.

THREE

Mither's Memories

There is nobody in this world who is not a historian. If you think about your own family background, you are being a historian. Your parents can in turn take you further back in time.

I tried this theory out with my mother when she came on a visit to Edinburgh in 1970, and filled several pages with notes about her own early days. Born in 1903 at a croft, Roadside of Auchenderran, Keith, she was brought up by her grannie, so that a lot of her knowledge was to do with the last quarter of the nineteenth century.

The croft was of about 60 acres, with a peat moss. There, her grannie cut peat with a peat spade that had a T-handle and an iron wing on the blade. It was worked down from the top of the bank. It was what was called a stumper or stump-spad farther down in Buchan, because you stamped it down with your foot. If you worked in from the face of the peat-bank, however, you worked with arms alone and in that case the spade was a breist-spad. Which type you used depended on the nature of the peat. As the peats at Auchenderran were cut, they were lifted off the blade and set up in little heapies of three, for drying. Some were barrowed home, but the main lot was taken home with her grannie's horse and cart. There was always a big peat stack for the winter. She sheiled off the grassy sods on top of the bank before she started digging the peat, and kept some of this to thatch the stack for the winter, first building it herself in the shape of a wee hoose. It wis aye biggit on a dry bit aboot the steadin, down beside the garden, which was a fine gairden o berries, an cabbage, an kail, an rasps, an rhubarb, an size (chives).

The placie had two cows for milking. The warm milk was taken into the milkhouse, which was built at the side of the house alongside the barn. Naturally a building so near the barn, and with the midden in the middle of the close, was not free of vermin, and grannie, whose husband had died of a shock, sitting in his armchair after supper, a whilie back, had learned to cope with wee moosies as with everything else on the farm. The technique was simple. She put a little dishie on to the milk shelf upside down – for example an aal cuppie withoot a hannle. She put a fairly large bowl against it, leaning on the very edge. The cheese bait was put on the flagstone close to the cup, and if a mouse happened to touch the cup, down came the bowl and the mouse was caught in this domestic deadfall trap. In the morning grannie came with a pail of water, and shuffled bowl and mouse together into it. She took care that the pail would be less than half-full to stop the mouse scrambling out.

Churning was done with a plump-churn with a lid, in the middle of which was an opening for the handle of the plumper that had a round wooden head bored with a number of holes. This was plunged up and down to make the butter, but in very hot weather, if the butter wouldn't come, grannie would whiles put in a grain of salt. On an average, three days' milk was kept for churning, and after churning, one of the treats was to get a piece, jist a bit of loaf spread wi a thoomfae o butter, stracht fae e churn on granny's thumb. When the butter came, you just washed your hands and lifted it out, then worked it in cold water till all the buttermilk was out of it. The buttermilk was put in a jar and kept for baking, or some of it could be drunk, or used to make buttermilk porridge (which nobody hears about these days).

The butter was made up into pounds and sold tae the mannie at cam roon wi the butter an egg cairt, the horse-drawn grocer's van, a long kind of cart with built partitions at each side and a full-length lid at each side, and a kind of runway along the middle that the mannie could move along. If ye bocht a loaf ye aye got a biscuit an if ye bocht a dizzen biscuits ye got een till't, one extra. The butter wasn't so much sold as bartered for groceries. At that time butter for sale had to have your name on it – grannie had a wooden stamp like a rose and another with her name, 'Stronach'. For the table at home the butter could be made up into ballies but that was only for visitors. Bairns got the job of scrubbing the butter dishes. The churn was washed out with hot water, as hot as ye could thole, and was set up on the dyke outside to dry.

My mother told me a lot about food and drink. The subject means a lot to all of us – and it is also a very good marker of social change.

Nowadays the seasons have nearly disappeared, because the pasteurising of milk lets it keep for much more than just over the weekend. But earlier on, milk supply was a seasonal thing, and that is one reason why other kinds of drinks were needed fin e kye wis eel. My mother's grannie made ale at that time. She got a bottle of stuff fae the chemist tae mak it, and a few bottles of ale would be the result. My mother, ever a teetotaller, never took it, and put sugar on her porridge instead – 'nae that I fancied it ower weel'. So it is clear enough that this ale was not made for social drinking, but as a substitute for milk on porridge and on anything else that needed to get a wash down.

Grannie eest take mak crudes and pit em in a cloot and hing em in a tree tae dry. She had a name for them – 'clootie cheese'. In Auchterless I have seen the same thing being done, but the name there was a 'hingie'. It was rare stuff to eat, with a clean white rind and a crumbly kind of fresh taste that was fine by itself, but went very well also with oatcakes. Ordinary cheese was also made in wooden vats pierced with holes to let the liquid ooze out, called 'chisels' about Auchenderran, but 'chessels' farther down the country. They were squeezed in a cheese press that had a screw on the top, so that the pressure could be increased every day.

For washing up, there was no water on tap. It had to be carried from a wallie, fine an caal, across the road.

The meal girnel was a plain painted square box – 'she keepit it ben in the milkhoose. I min on hit' ('hit' for 'it' is another Keith characteristic). First the corn was taken to the mill to be ground into meal, then it was taken home, and pressed well into the girnel with a tattie chapper. It wisna jist e meal at cam hame, it wis e pron (bran or husks) tee. It wis chappit in amon e tatties till e hens. The dist also came home for the hens. This wis just like styoo (dust).

'Pron' is actually a name found from Caithness down to Perthshire along the Highland line, as a dialect word that comes from the Gaelic *pronn,* meaning bran. The lowland equivalent is sids, the particles of bran sifted out from the meal at the mill, but whether pron or sids, nothing was wasted and you used it to feed the hens and turned some of it into sowens. The system was to soak the pron for a day or two, and all the mealy stuff sank like a kind of sludge to the bottom. Syne ye syed it, put in saat – an spice if ye likit – an bilet it up. Some folk pat fusky amon't fin they were haein a meal-an-ale at the eyn o the hairst. They made a fairly liquid dish, which was put in a basin with a ladle, and with this you filled your bowl.

The daily routine was fairly well fixed. Rising time was about 5 to 6 o'clock. The horses were cleaned before you had your breakfast, sometime between 7 and 8 o'clock. It was always porridge as the mainstay, though my mother's uncle would take brose now and again. It was always water porridge for breakfast, with tea and breid and milk, though for dinner you could get milk porridge. There wis aye cheese an jam on e table, and a bit loaf.

A foreneen piece wis nae bit jist in e hairst time. There was no concept of having morning tea at Roadside of Auchenderran. Dinner time was about 12 to 1 o'clock. There wis broth files or tattie soup, pea soup maist days, except maybe in e simmer. In summer you had a bowlie o yirnt milk and oatcakes for yer puddin, sometimes that alone for the whole dinner with oatcakes and milk after that if wanted. Broth or soup with oatcakes after was often your dinner. Every so often, there was meat – files sheep's heid broth. Vans didn't carry meat at that time. Grannie sometimes bought a half heart from the butcher in Keith. Stovies were fairly regular, chappit tatties wi size throwe em. Sometimes you got salt herring, and also dried fish and mustard. Or there was chappit kail made with cream, a handful of meal and a pinch of carbonate of soda, boiled in a pot and chappit in the same pot. Just the curly leaves were used, and this was a meal in itself. Neeps and neep brose wis aften a denner on e stormy days, bit ye need a drappie gweed milk jist tae pit em doon richt. Ye never made tea at dinner time.

Supper on ordinary nights was often porridge, or fried tatties and an egg, often a duck's egg, though this was always boiled. You got tea if you wanted, and this was about 6 o'clock. On Sunday night, oatcakes an crudes were common. Clootie dumplins were made quite often for supper or for dinner.

To end the day, you got a bed-piece, tea or a bowl of milk, and the bairns got a cup of milk and a farden biscuit.

Whiles there was a treat after the cow calved, in the shape of a dish of calfie's cheese. My mother made this sometimes at Pitglassie as well. It was queer kind o stuff, ye baith liked it and ye didna. It was sweet and it was spicy, but it also had a soft texture. When you put a spoonful into your mouth you could press it into a kind of mush with your tongue and it made you in a strange kind of way think of the calf that wasn't getting its full nourishment. Calfie's cheese was made with the very first milk that came off after calving. It was put in a flat dishie, sugar was stirred through it, and if you liked you could sprinkle cinnamon on top. Then you put it into the oven in the kitchen range and just left it till it firmed up. But if you didn't have an oven, like at Auchenderran, it was put in a pan by the fireside, which was just a big open one with two brickies at the side. When the stuff was ready, you could eat it hot or cold.

Fit else did ma mither tell's aboot the place? Well, washing was a job for Monday. Water was carried from the well and filled into a big iron pot over the fire. This was why the big swey was so handy. When the water boiled you just swung the pot out and then you could lift it off without stretching over the bleezin eizels, or else you could just lave out the water. Grannie had two wooden stands with a tub on each of them. She started washing in one tub and then put the clothes into clean water in the other. She had a hard board in a wooden frame with a zincy kind o a middle. She used Sunlight soap that came in long bars that were cut up and laid on a shelf to harden. The washing was put on the grass on the green to bleach, and when it came to hanging things on the line, she had a gweed puckle widden pegs bocht fae haakers at cam roon e door. They were made o twa bits o stick wi a tin band roon them an a tackie tae haad them. Syne up geed e claes pole, an there wis yer fine Monday washin for aa tae see.

Hawkers didn't only sell clothes pegs, but also wee heather pot scrubbers, safety preens, needles, tape, tin pails, tin bowlies and a lot besides.

The house had a rough cement kitchen floor, but ben the hoose in the room, in the little closet off the kitchen, and in the two rooms up the stair, the floors were of wood. You usually went to bed about 9 o'clock, not just to save light, but also because you got up early in the morning. On bigger farms that had chaamers, the chaamer lads were out of the house by 9 o'clock in the evening, but whether or no they geed tae their beds then was anither question.

Christmas is a new-fangled affair, and little attention was paid to it at Auchenderran. No decorations were put up, and the only time you hung up your stockings for presents was at Hogmanay. There was no word of bairns going around at Hogmanay with their faces blackened, asking for pieces, though they did this in Auchterless and I was one of them.

The main nights when folk gathered were at the end o hairst. My mother's uncle Jimmie Stronach was a great melodeon player. Fowk wid came in aboot, bit the bairns hid tae tak a back seat. They had to wait their turn for their tea until the visitors had theirs. There wid maybe be a bit o dancin, a sing-song, and sometimes fiddlin. Her uncle's favourite tune was 'Sweet Rothesay Bay'.

There's still a fyow orrals tae tidy up aboot the things ma mither tellt's.

First of all, there was her grannie. I got no description of

65

what she looked like, though I have an old photograph of her, a sweet-faced lady whose image is a wee bit spoiled by colour tinting, which makes her look as if her cheeks were covered with rouge – a thing, I'm quite certain, she would never have worn. But I did hear about her clothes. For daily work, she wore a wincey apron (pronounced 'aapren'), and if visitors came, she would put on a fancier one. She always had long skirts, which must have been warm if any heavy work was being done, and there wis a pooch (I've heard it caaed a 'grannie pooch') geed in doon the seam. When working on the land she might wear man's boots, wi a divot o strae in em because they were too big, but when she went from home she was quite the lady, with button-up-the-side boots that you had to fasten with a button hook.

My mother's grannie died in about 1927 at the age of 78, and is buried in Bellie Kirkyard. My mother's mother, my grannie, died at Wetwards in Drumblade on 6 April, 1940, and is buried in Gartly Kirkyard. When as a wee loon I lived at Brideswell Cottages in Drumblade, I would walk up the burn side and throwe the parks tae Drumblade, where I liked to catch my grannie on baking day. She used a rolling pin with grooves all round it for making her oatcakes, so that when the cyaaks were ready, they were also covered with ridges. It was her that would take a scoop of freshly made butter on the edge of her thumb and clart it on before handing it to me. This was the thoom piece, pure manna for a hungry loon.

To end the notes from my mother, here is just a wee mixture. Hay was mown with the reaper (there was no binder then), turned with forks or graips to win and then put into hooicks. They were left for a while, and then were teen hame an biggit intill a ruckie at the back. The cornyard at Auchenderran was at the back of the barn. For each there was a circle of stones that served as the ruck foon. Only corn, i.e. oats, was grown. The rucks were theekit an raipit, and my mother used to twine the raips ben the byre, using a thraacrook. Grannie was fairly good at lettin oot the strae. Neeps were sown thicker than they were later, an nott mair hyowin. There was a timmer cairt shed, an a widden hen-hoose biggit on till't. There was space for two carts.

That's what I got from my mother, an gin I'd been mair eident I mith a gotten a lot mair.

This bittie's tae dae wi ma grandfather on ma father's side. Hiv ye ivver heard o an 'overlay'? If ye hinna, ye mith ken't as a 'pitowerlie' or a 'legs-ower-im'. They were made by local black-smiths, and never manufactured and distributed centrally, so there were plenty of individual shapes. They all had handles, with a hole in the end for hanging them up. Some were open-ended, like a tuning fork, about a foot-and-a-half long by four inches wide. One like this used by my mother at Pitglassie came from a house in Torrie Street, Huntly, so you could get them in the towns as well as in the countryside. Another one I've seen was shaped like an elongated oval, and a third was a closed rectangle. It was made by my grandfather, blacksmith at Kinmundy and later in Aberdeen (he passed his apprenticeship in 1879). Div ye ken fit it is yet? Weel, it's jist a thing ye lay ower the tap o an open range tae haad up pots an pans ower e fire, or files tae keep up e lid o a pot tae had it on bilin ower.

Noo, this is a simple an handy thing, bit it means a lot. For one thing, it goes with the days when pots and pans for cooking had come to have flat bottoms, and that in turn goes with kitchen ranges. It's a stage in a long development. Farrer back, there wis fires in the middle o e fleer, bit they dee't oot lang seen in the North-East, an aifter at — maybe aboot twa hunner eer seen —

widden hingin lums set against e inside o e gale come in. I've seen a lot o em as I was gaan aboot e place in the 1950s and '60s, bit I doot ey're fyow an far atween noo. The fireplace could be at the level of the floor, and then very quickly there began to be hobs at the sides, with the iron bars of a grate between and an ash pit or an ash pan below. The hobs were handy for kettles and pots, and as often as not, there was also an iron swey. The swey was hinged against the cheek of the fireplace.

As long as there was no grate, you could manage fine with round-bottomed, three-legged pots, and usually there were several in different sizes. They had to be hung over the fire. But as soon as you started to have a grate, with hobs at the side, you could get a different set of kitchen equipment and that was when the flat bottoms came in. So the pitowerlie marks a stage in the development of the kitchen.

An aafa lot o e places I kent hid open ranges, including ma mither's hoose, used for cooking as well as heating until things like the Rippingille stove came along between the wars, using 'clean' fuels like paraffin. I min fine on the changed smell o e kitchen. There wis nae jist the fine bakin smells, bit the yoam o het paraffin as weel. Some of the bigger ranges were closed on top of the fire box, so that you cooked on top of a hot plate. I suppose you can say that the coming of the kitchen range was a real kitchen revolution. The cast-iron range, with an oven at one side and often a boiler for hot water at the other, began to spread after about the 1780s, and places like the Carron Ironworks at Falkirk made them to suit every size of kitchen and pocket. They were sold through the local ironmongers' shops. They were good pieces of design, and they made kitchens much cleaner (though you still had to light the fire in the morning, and I remember very well listening from my bedroom to my mother raking out the ashes with the poker rattling on the bars of the grate, before setting the fire with twisted pages of the 'P & J' (*Press & Journal*), some kinnlin and lumpies o coal – then I'd get up when the kitchen was warm). But they also brought in the days, in Victorian times, of all the wide range of kitchen equipment that we had never had before, and that included the modest pitowerlie.

FOUR

Mabel Smith's Stories

My French teacher at Turriff Secondary School (as it was in my time, before it became upsides down with Inverurie and turned into an Academy) was Miss Mary B. Smith, known to her friends as Mabel, and I am glad to say that I became one. She was a great source of inspiration, and though she officially taught me French, she encouraged the knowledge of other languages as well, and was never slow to produce grammar books and readers to whet the appetite.

When I first knew her she lived with her parents at Mill of Delgaty, and later she moved into Turriff, where she had a splendid garden, and spent a lot of time noting down fairlies, partly at my suggestion and partly because she wanted to anyway. She had a remarkable memory and a fine sense of fun, and inherited a great deal of local lore from her parents.

Here is some of what I got from her directly, and from her notebooks.

It was said of a child, that 'if ye spoke afore ye traivelt ye wis gaan tae be an aafa leear'. To 'traivel' is a good word for to walk, still common enough in the North-East, though it is not only a Buchan word, but is known throughout Scotland.

And thinking of 'leears', there is the well-known comment, 'the biggest leear gets the biggest cheer'. Mabel explained that this would be said to a visitor coming into the kitchen and being asked to sit down in the wooden armchair.

One that enshrines the rural philosophy developed by years of

70

subsistence living is 'I'll tak it atween me an want'. This was said –
or sometimes thought, for the sake of politeness – when offered
something to eat or drink that you took, even if you didn't like it,
when nothing else was available. The same background of necessary thrift may be seen in slowness to pay bills: 'I'll pey ye fin aa
man peys idder', in other words on doomsday.

Her mother would gather and cut up dandelion leaves, as many
as she could get, to put into the hens' pot, along with tatties, meal,
etc. It was the habit to leave the hens' pot near the fire, which was
in all night, so that the hennies could get the food warm. It seemed
to suit their taste.

An his onybody ivver telt ye ye wis jist a perfect wick? That's
what might be said of a boy who was a bit over-active and
mischievous. It's not too common a word, and it was good to
be able to record it as recently as 1985.

I asked Mabel Smith for information on the eating habits of her
folk when they lived near Fraserburgh, and she told me a lot.
About 1902–1909, a married man would get meal, milk and tatties
from the farmer, as well as coal and peats. This was very much
their diet, and as cottars at Leys of Auchmacoy, their daily fare was
something like this:

On weekdays, her father had brose, tea, and bread and butter,
her mother had the same except for the brose (she liket neither
brose nor porridge, like a hullock o ither fowk that widna admit
till't), and Mabel herself and her sister Elsie had porridge, with tea,
bread and butter. Sunday was different. There was no brose or
porridge, but they got their oatmeal ration with oatcakes, backed
up with bread and tea. It's aye interestin tae tak note o e different
diets o the men and the weemen.

Dinner in the middle of the day was mostly tatties an saat. Beef and broth was the Sunday dinner, if someone had brought beef from the butcher's, two and a half miles away. This meant yavel broth on the Monday. A yavel crap wis e second crap in succession teen fae a park, so tae think o second day's broth as yavel wis gweed fairmin logic. I've even heard them (broth wis aye 'they') caad yavellers. Nae dialect's iver deid fin ye can mak up wirds in't. If there happened to be any beef left, it would make a dish of stovies, and on one day there could be tattie soup. Sometimes there could be a rabbit, for her father was good with aiming a stone, or maybe a pigeon if one of the single men was lucky with the gun, or an old hen or cock.

The two girls had their dinner kept warm for when they came home from school, where they just had a piece, a thick slice of loaf spread with syrup or trycle, but very seldom jam.

The fare was improved when one of her father's sisters came on a visit, for she could make even the simplest dishes taste better. She would get a half ox-head, which wasn't scraped to the bone in these days and make pottit heid, sealed in 2lb stone jars, and then heated up and made into soup.(It was more commonly eaten cold.) Ye couldna keep the jars ower lang. Whiles she got an ox heart which she stuffed and stewed. And sometimes they had milk rice soup, though for some reason Mabel's father widna hae milk barley soup. Another time the food was a bittie better was when someone came looking for lodgings. Mabel remembered two quarrymen who stayed, and a trapper, who brought in a good supply of rabbits.

Pudding was nearly always rice pudding with syrup because her father liked it. Enough was made for two days at a time. – and so you can see how the man's tastes could condition the kind of diet a household had. In summer there was stewed rhubarb – at hame I aye likit tae watch the milk curdlin as ye poored it on – and on birthdays and special days there were clootie dumplins.

For supper at six o'clock it wis back tae the oatmeal, with porridge, sometimes milk porridge with sugar or syrup, or milk brose. But her father had his own likes and stuck to cold milk pudding. When available they had kail brose followed by chappit kail (only after the kail had got a touchie of frost), or cabbage brose with chappit cabbage, or neep brose (the neeps were swedes), and chappit neeps. There were home-baked scones for tea as long as they lasted after the once-a-week baking.

When the twa quines were quite young, they would get the taps o their parents' boiled eggs. Later they got one between them, cut through the middle, bit maist o e eggs wis sellt tae the merchant in return for groceries. But there was a whole egg for breakfast at Pace, Easter Sunday.

In the early 1900s, the fish cairt wid whiles come roon till e cotter hoose at Leys o Auchmacoy, though nae very aften. Then they wid hae fried herrin, kippers or yalla haddock for tea – that was the last meal of the day for the whole family. Fish made a fine variation on the diet, but there were other possibilities too. For example, saps could be made instead of the perpetual porridge, once in a while, made of loaf and sugar and heated milk. Though Mabel Smith's father couldna stand them, he fyles hid tae thole. At ae place faar he'd been caain oot muck – een o e hardest jobs ye can get on a fairm – he got saps ower aften for eez denner, an wis ravenous or supper time. In the spring there wid be teuchits' eggs, gathered from the tilled fields. Teuchits or peesees or wallapies (in Morayshire), it's aa e same bird, an it's jist richt fine tae hear em an see em on a spring day. I eest tae tak some eggs masel, in company wi ither loons, an bile them in an aal tinnie ower a fire made at the edge o e wid, an boy! they tastit fine, though the antrin een wid turn oot tae be gorblet.

Mabel was convinced that meals depended on the cook and on the likes and dislikes of the family members, and especially of the head of the house, though in the kitchen whether that was father or mother was debatable. I've mentioned the saps already, but other taboos were chappit tatties and tatties boiled with milk and onions, and ground rice pudding, 'because Father would't have them'. Another thing was that 'Mother didn't like cooking, also she had some idea that it was sinful to pander to one's stomach, maybe just to cover up the fact that she wasn't interested'.

A baker's van came once a week, when bread and a few biscuits were bought. The biscuits were as big as a saucer – they've maistly geen doonhill since then! – and Mabel and her sister would get one between them. There were no cups of tea between meals then, though the girls did sometimes get a piece on a Saturday, a slice of bread spread with syrup – which I have heard called 'the poor man's honey'. In-betweens have become a regular habit now, and I'll never forget the time I visited friends in Shetland. At their house in Scalloway, you got a cup of tea in bed, tea with your breakfast, tea mid-morning, tea after your dinner, tea with your tea, tea with your 'eight o' clockses', and tea with supper before you went to bed. This was very different from Leys o Auchmaccoy.

The worst day for the children was Sunday. As Mabel wrote: 'I had to walk about three miles to Sunday School, crossing the Ythan by boat to Logie Buchan Church. After Sunday School we went out to the churchyard where many grown-ups had arrived for church. Then we went back indoors with them, returning home after the service at great speed to keep up with the adults. If both parents had been to church it was an age till dinner was ready, the fire was out or nearly so – the fireplace a poor affair with binks, no oven'.

They got a huge kebbock of cheese twice a year from their father's mother, and this was good kitchie at teatime, especially the summer cheese. Ye'll aa ken fit kitchie is? It's the North-East form of 'kitchen', in the sense of something eaten or drunk along with plain food to give it a wee bit of taste. It disna need tae be sweet – though it often would be nowadays – an could jist be milk tae yer porrich, or butter an cheese tae yer breid. Weel, fowk were richt glaid o a bit o kitchie in the hard days o the first fyow ears o the 1900s.

Things got a bittie better for the Smiths between 1905 and 1915, when they were at the Home Farm, Philorth. Maybe wages were higher. John Smith was cattleman at the farm. They got as much separated milk as they wanted, and Mrs Smith was paid for milking and looking after the poultry, though they weren't allowed to keep any. This meant that there were no eggs and no old hens to be eaten or boiled in the broth pot, though the manager would often give them badly-shaped eggs. Nooadays hens must be trained tae lay sma, medium or large, ilky een perfect, bit nae then! Being close to the Broch, they often had fish for dinner or for tea. In the house there was a kitchen range with an oven, and Mabel was encouraged to bake in it. At that time she had bought a wooden spoon for a penny tae steer e mixters. It was still being used in 1965, so it had paid for itself many times over by then. At Christmas they always got enormous bits of meat when a Highland stirk was killed and parted out amongst the folk. Mabel said this was the best beef she had ever tasted. The gamies (gamekeepers) were generous wiith rabbits, and soft fruit could be bought from the gardener. The family bought sugar by the hundredweight until the War broke out, and flour by the bow (boll). After the War they never started bulk buying again.

In 1932 the family climbed a hackie up and moved to the 10-
acre croft at Mill o Delgaty, Turriff. The daily diet followed the
same pattern that I've been telling you about, but there was a far
greater variety of vegetables and soft fruit grown in the garden.
Bones were bought for soup. Mr Smith liked to 'clean' the
marrow-bones, by cracking them and sucking out the juice.
None of the family was keen on mutton or pork, apart from
bacon or sausages whiles for tea. But though the later meals had
more variety than in the old days at Leys o Achmacoy, breakfast
remained much the same, just brose or porridge and tea, with tea
alone on Sundays.

Up to 1939, things were better and there were all sorts of changes
in the diet. For example, semolina pudding took the place of rice,
and was eaten with all kinds of jam on it, or stewed fruit when it
was in season. Otherwise apples or dried fruit could be bought.
Forbye, the habit of drinking a cup of tea after dinnertime had
come in, and there was a cup of tea with a biscuit at bedtime.
There was plenty of cheese and jams, and no scarcity of eggs,
chickens, meal and potatoes. They now had a decent cooker with
an oven, and a greater variety of dishes was made – pea-soup, lentil
soup, skink soup, various casserole dishes for meat, fish and
puddings. Cheese was cheap, and a Danish Blue of 4 or 5lbs
could be bought for 5/-. Even so, it was impossible to make money
and it was still a case of scraping.

World War II brought harder times again. Tea at dinnertime
stopped, and there was no 'bed-piece'. There wasn't even much
loaf. Meals in general were poor and the habit developed of having
snacks between times to keep them going. Maybe it was the War
that started this habit, which is well known now still, throughout
the country, not only for farm folk but also for tradesmen and
workers of all kinds.

And on Sundays, for a treat, they would get toast, butter, sugar and cinnamon. As Mabel's father would say, treats like that should be 'jist at Eel (Yule) an Pace (Easter) an at aa high times'.

If ye hidna got an oven in the kitchen, and just an open peat fire, ye could still bake fruit cakes. Ye hid tae hae a cast-iron oven pot. It was very solid, had a flat bottom, and a great heavy lid. It had three legs, bit it wisna aafa heich. When it was being used, it sat not too close in to the fire, and hot 'quiles' were laid on the lid so that the heat went down from the top as well. Noo, some folk wid say ye hid tae shove the pot weel intae the side o the peat-fire, bit Mabel Smith's auntie or grannie at Hythie made cakes in the pot oven, so they hid their ain experience. There's aye a wye tae dee something! An if ye wintit tae roast meat, ye could dee't in metal trays ower e fire, though the fire had tae be bonny an reed for this jobbie.

As for this word 'quiles', it means glowing embers of coal, peat, wood etc. and it is the same word as 'coal'. In the dialect there was aye a difference atween 'coal' that wisna lit or wis jist beginnin tae bleeze, an the 'quyles' that were a later stage – jist fine for bakin, or roastin a bittie o cheese an makkin a fine yoam in e kitchen.

Here's a fyow mair samples o fit they hid tae ate aboot 1902–9. Skirlie was one. I once mentioned the word to one of my daughters and she gave a good skraich, so I had to explain to her the meaning of this Buchan word. It is oatmeal, pepper and salt, maybe an onion, cooked in as much fat as it will absorb. The Smiths occasionally had skirlie if somebody had bought suet. If they had bought more beef than usual, the butcher would clap a bit suet on top for nothing. This, of course, was in the good old days, when you would usually get something extra with a fair order. There was the butcher's suet, and the baker would give biscuits, and the grocer a twist of sweets or pins. Ye didna need loyalty cards then! Bit ither things were different tee. Ye didna ask for a pound o, say, skink, bit it was sixpence worth or a shillin's worth o this or that, as ivery penny hid tae be coontit, an the butcher wid hae tae be sure tae cut fully mair than the pun o fitiver ye'd asked.

Then there was salt butter. Mabel's aunt (Fanny) on her father's side sometimes stayed with them, and she taught her mother tae saut butter for e winter. The best time tae dee't wis hairst – September and October. The butter was worked for a spell, several days on end, salt and saltpetre being slowly added, then it was pressed hard by hand into a crock. When full, the crock top was covered with several layers of butter paper, then brown paper, and all firmly tied down. The strength o a man's hand cam in handy here an this wis a job her father did. Later when the crock was opened, you scraped out the butter with a spoon, making it curl as it came. Ye didna mak it intae pats as ye wid dee wi fresh butter.

A pleasant change – if you liked it – was peasemeal brose. The Smiths had it now and again when the merchant had a supply of peasemeal. It was eaten with syrup and creamy milk. Another thing you could get in some houses was a mealy dumpling tied in a cloot and boiled in soup.

Bit noo, we'll finish aff wi pop. Aunt Fanny taught Mabel's mother how to make 'ginger beer' from yeast and sugar. It certainly fizzed, and it was the grown-ups that drank it. The two girls were delighted when a cork flew and the stuff frothed out, and mother rushed to get a bowl to catch it. They hoped they might get a sup in the by-going.

It was that same aunt that introduced them to putting ground or whole cloves into rhubarb jam, which was the only jam they had unless they fell in with some wild rasps. Though goods were scant, folk learned to make them tasty.

When the Smiths went to Home Farm, Frendraught, in 1921, there happened to be no salt left in the house, so Father sent the loon to the shop at Corse for half-a-stone. The shopkeeper was quite upset. 'I'll gie ye a pun', said he. 'Gin aabody wis to seek a half-steen, I'd seen hae naething left.'

A lot o fowk likit beremeal porridge an beremeal scones. You used to be able to get the meal at Norman Deans' shop in Turra. He used to sell peasemeal – pizzers – as well, and once showed Mabel Smith the bag it came in, from France. Apparently French peasemeal was the best, and poorer quality was no treat. Beremeal and pizzers, like sowens, were supposed to be good for folk with stomach troubles, and in fact I remember paying a visit to a croft in Caithness once, where two ladies lived by themselves and did their own baking. Beremeal scones were always on the menu, and one of the sisters told me: 'I just take a bit of bere-meal scone in the morning and it keeps me right all day'.

In districts nae ower far fae e coast, the fish-cairt or the fishwife wid come roon, and the farm folk would buy hard dried fish. 'Hiv ye ony dry fish, Missus?' the coorse loons wid say. 'Aye.' 'Ah weel, gie them a drink.' The fish, dried ling, was used a lot for dinners and teas. At Mabel's grandfather's house, it was stored in the loft. The ling was two or three feet long, and Mabel and her sister would have to hold one end while their grandmother skinned it. Then it was cut up into 4-inch squares, boiled, and served with tatties and mustard sauce for dinner, and later on cold for tea. If there was a big family, you had to make such dishes go as far as you could. So the trick was to redd the fish of bones, and then chap it through the tatties to make it bulk more. Milk could be added to it, and this was the time-honoured dish called hairy tatties. Mabel said they hardly ever saw hard fish till they went to Philorth.

Anither wye o hainin was to hae a meal-in. Or if there was a bakin day and nae much time tae mak a full denner, ye micht get a meal-in tee. It was common enough if you had plenty of separated milk, and all you did was to get a bowl of milk and crumble into it a piece of hot oatcakes. I've tried it, and it's very pleasant. Some folk heated the milk and added cold oatcakes, but I never could abide warm milk so that system was not for me.

In fact, meals were often conditioned by the work of the day. Friday was baking day, a forenoon's work. Monday was washing day, so second day's broth – yavel broth – was handy for dinner. Churning day was about Wednesday. On Saturday the whole house got a good redd-up. Spoons, knives and forks had to be cleaned and polished, then they were plotted in boiling water to get rid of the cleaning stuff. There wisna much interest in makkin a big denner that day.

Here are some of the occasional meals that Mabel mentioned. Hotch potch was eaten about once in summer, when vegetables were at their best. You just boiled a little of anything that was available as soup, without any meat. Barfit broth was something similar, made at any time when vegetables were to be had, with barley and split peas for thickening but no meat.

At the houses of relatives, she sometimes got fried liver and onions for tea. They never had this at home, as her father couldn't stand the smell of it. Liver, like all offal, was cheap then, but not very widely appreciated.

The kinna mait ye got on a fairm or craft dependit a lot on the work o the day an the time o ear. A gweed example's calfie's cheese, or new cheese, as Mabel Smith ca'd it. She hid a great aunt at a dairy fairm, an it wis there she tastit new cheese. Appeerently they didna get it at hame. It was made from the first milking after a cow calved, sugar and spices were added, especially cinnamon (my ain mither eest tae mak it, an she sprinklet e cinnamon on tap – see page 64), and then it was put in its dish into a cool oven till it set. It was soft stuff, eaten cold as a pudding.

Another dish was yirnt milk. It was best made with milk still warm from the cow, with rennet, and this was much better than with warmed-up milk. Mabel's mither likit it, bit nae er faither. They sometimes had it as pudding, with sugar, served in separate bowls, bit it wisna much good if ye were richt hungry. I've eaten yirnt milk often enough at home too, and I remember it especially in combination with a quarter of new-baked oatcakes. It seemed to bring out the fine mealy flavour. Some folk would eat it with a spoonful of home-made raspberry or strawberry jam

Of course, there was also the very common habit with farm servants of finishing off a meal with 'milk an breid', for a basin of milk and oatcakes was always on the table. Another thing you would usually get on the table was 'a fluggin o seerup' tae spread on yer piece. If ye wis a canny hoosewife, ye'd keep e jarrie o seerup aside e kitchen fire durin e day, so it wid rin thin an ye couldna spread on ower much.

Hiv ye iver heard o buttermilk breid? In the days afore National Health dentists (an they're gettin scarce enyeuch again!) aaler fowk micht hae fyow teeth, an that wis fin buttermilk breid cam in handy. It wis oatcakes jist made wi buttermilk instead o watter and meltit fat. They turned out thickish, not very hard, and rich tasting. Mabel liked them, even though she had her teeth, but the rest of the family didn't care so much for them. Her mother made girdle scones with buttermilk too. And buttermilk was a favourite cooling drink in the summertime.

There was always plenty of oatmeal, because the cottars got a generous allowance, and many of them sold part of it to the grocer in the early 1900s. If the family was big, this was necessary, because they could hardly avoid being in or near debt. No doubt, though, the grocer would get the best of the bargain, and it was just a matter of bad luck if there was a bad harvest and the meal tasted vile. At Philorth, the Smith family had meal from tattie corn, a blackish corn that made lovely porridge though folk didn't like the look of it.

Meal had another use, too, and this is one I'd never heard of till Mabel told me. It was for preserving eggs. Mabel's aunt would sometimes rub an egg with butter and bury it in a pailful of meal. It would keep like this for several weeks, and then the meal would be used to feed the chickens.

When the Smiths were at Mains of Slains, 1900–1901, they were not far from the coast, and so they had a good chance of getting fish. They had lovely cod or ling with their tatties. This was a favourite of her father, but her mother preferred yellow smoked haddock, kippers and siclike. She thought white fish was tasteless. They often had Collieston speldins for their tea. They were whitings dried on the rocks, and grilled on a wire contraption over a red fire, then put in a bowl of boiling water to soften them and extract some of the salt. Then they were dried in a cloth and eaten. A lot o work! It was a Collieston fishwife called Sarah (pronounced 'sarra') who brought them.

Size, chives, were used a lot to make dishes tasty, things like chappit tatties and egg-dishes. Carvy, carraway seeds, were popular to flavour cakes and biscuits and could even be put into cheese when it was being made. It made the cheese flavoursome, but harder at the same time.

Noo for a Hogmanay story. Fin Mabel wis twa an a half, her mither bocht a fruit loaf aff a baker's van. She got half-a-slice at teatime, a broonie kinna loaf wi a fyow raisins. Then as she says: 'Next morning Mother poked me awake far too early for my liking, as soon as Father had departed for the farm, before 6 am, and expected me to be enthusiastic over my stocking, which contained an orange, an apple, a whole slice of fruit loaf cut in two and a penny. I distinctly remember thinking the bread was strangely like what I'd had the day before, rousing my first suspicions about Santa Claus'.

Noo we can sit back an listen till a fyow o Mabel's stories. There wis the first horseman at Middletack. Him an e fairmer were inclined to spar, though they wid niver actually faa oot. In e winter time, if e fairmer got Tam lowsin ten meenits afore time, he wid order im aff for anither load o neeps. Tam wid haad till e neep-park for five meenits, syne turn back an lowse. Ae day in spring, Tam wis tellt tae gang till e shim. Tae get a swingle-tree tae yoke e shim, e'd tae gang throwe e hens' run. Be ill chance, he let oot a hen. The fairmer noticed this on his wye back till e hoose, an shoutit, 'Pit in at hen afore ye gyang awa!' Tam tied his horse till a tree an startit tae walk ahin e hen. Half an oor later e fairmer cam oot. 'Hiv ye nae gotten at hen in yet?' 'Na', said Tam, 'bit I'm weerin er oot.'

There wis a man caa'd John Aden. His wife died suddenly ae day aboot noon, fin he wis haein a day in the moss, castin peats. Neepers cam till e moss tae tell im fit hid happened. 'At's a curst skyte', said John, 'bit I'll be hame at even.'

Seein we're on this tack, there's e tale o an elderly crafter. His wife hid deet. The day o the funeral wis stormy. This wis in the twenties, fin cars werena very common. A fairmer geed e aal man a lift till Ythanwells Kirkyard. Fin ey got back hame again, e aal man said till e fairmer, fair teen wi imsel: 'Man! I hiv enjoyed at hurl!'

Mabel Smith's stories hiv a lot o the atmosphere o the North-East in em, bit neen o them are coorse, though there's plenty o coorse stories aboot.

Aboot the turn o the century, the mistress at the fairm wis tellin Feel Willie tae tak a basketfae o eggs till e merchant's. 'Noo, mind, dinna sell em unless ye get ten pence a dizzen for em.' Fin Willie cam back, e basket wis teem. 'Foo did ye get on, Willie?', she speert. 'I see ye've gotten ten pence for em.' 'Aye', said Willie, fair delighted. 'They were gyaan tae gie me a shillin, bit I screwed em doon tae ten pence'.

The same Willie, like ithers o his kind, hid a great appetite. Fin he cried in by e shop ae evenin, the merchant got im tae buy some reid herrins. He said Willie could easy cook them imsel in the chaamer, for 'they only nott a look at e fire'. On the wye hame, Willie saa a bleeze in e distance, sae he took a herrin fae e package an held it up in e direction o the fire. Be ill luck, he let it faa. Scrabblin aboot for't in e dark, he happent tae pick up a frog. It objectit. 'Na,na', said Willie, 'ye've seen e fire an ye'll hae tae go.'

Jimmy'd haen a tirin day in the moss, an tae croon aa, Sally his pony laired an couldna be got oot. He held up the road till e souter's at Cortiecram, thinking there'd be sure tae be a fyow customers gaithert in the evenin. There wis sae much talk fin Jimmy gaed in that he didna like tae mention his predicament, an e jist sat doon wi the rest. Later on, a lot later, fin e company startit tae brak up, Jimmy pluckit up courage and mentiont fit wis wrang. 'Gweed sakes', said e souter, 'Foo did ye nae tell's fin ye cam in?' 'Oh', said Jimmy, 'she winna be awa.'

Mabel had a story about Maggie the fishwife's first sight of a train on the Broch line. This is what she said: 'I wis near the Philorth Brig fin I saa e dirty reek o er comin. She ran an I ran, I ran an she ran an we met at the Brig. I fell doon caal deid, an nae ae thing gaed ower ma haase for a week'.

The next item is not much of a story, but it gives a vivid picture of a thatched house and its hingin lum. You would think that with the wide opening, the house would be pretty draughty. It was the time of a snowstorm. The snow reached right to the lum of the smith's thackit hoose an wis frozen hard. This gies ye an idea o the big storms we eest tae get, tee. A lad caad Jockie Robertson wis oot for a Sunday aifterneen walk, an he wis able tae gang on the tap o the snaa richt up till e lum. He lookit doon, an saa e smith, Dippins (Mabel thinks his name was Dipthingham) an his wife Kirsty sittin on ilky side o e fireplace. Canny as ye like, Jockie drappit a hanfae o snaa doon e lum. 'Dyod, umman', said Dippins, 'it's surely gyaan tae be fresh.' 'I'll gie ye fresh', thocht Jockie, an e heaved doon an airmfae o snaa. Bit fin e heard e clatter o the tae-pot on the steen fleer, he thocht he'd better tak tae his heels.

Marriage is not always a straightforward matter. Mabel Smith found this out from one of her former pupils, Nan. When Nan left school, she took up nursing, and always greeted Mabel cheerfully when she was home on leave. One time she confessed she was to be getting married, and took Mabel along the street a bit to meet her intended, a local farmer.

Fin Mabel met er in a neeberin toon a filie aifter, Nan didna jist look aa that happy, bit Mabel didna let on she noticed an jist asked: 'Are you enjoying being a farmer's wife, better than a nurse?' Nan hesitatit, an syne said in a laigh voice: 'Weel, Miss Smith, it's like this, it's jist a change'.

Mabel, being a teacher, had a fund of school stories, which she would tell with a wicked chuckle. The teacher was talking of houses to a new class of infants. 'Do any of you know the name of the pig's house?' No answer. 'Come on now, I'm sure someone knows where the pig stays.' Up shot Tibby's hand. 'I ken, in e midden.' 'Oh, no, the pig has a nice little house, and it's called a sty.' 'I'm nae carin onywye', muttered Tibby, 'oor een bides in e midden.'

That gives a wee hint of the living conditions of pigs in earlier days, and another story says something about wartime conditions, when oranges were a bittie hard to come by. Five-year-old Lena was waiting for Mabel one dinnertime when she was coming out of school. 'I've had chickenpox', she said. 'I wisna here fin ye geed some o them an orange'. 'We'll need to see about that', said Mabel, and she went into the nearby grocer's shop to see if he had any oranges for children. She bought a few, and gave one to Lena, who stuffed it into her pocket. 'Why not eat it, Lena, since you wanted it so much?' Lena made no response, but after a minute looked up and said: 'I'll easy haad anither een in the ither pooch'.

Anither school denner time on a warm simmer day, e country scholars wis sittin on a sinny bank, tae ate their piece. Ae lad wis openin up his package in a canny wye, sayin slow bit loud: 'I winner fit she's geen me the day?' As he got inside his package, his nose geed in e air: 'Cheese – cheese! Chee-eese again! Dis e bugger think I'm a moose?'

Anither story had mair o a university ring. It happened aboot e First World War, an it's a gweed illustration o the sayin, 'fit ye dinna ken disna hurt ye'. Two girl students were walking along King Street in Aberdeen in the summer of 1914. They happened to notice, through a grating opening on a basement, an apprentice baker who was filling split cookies with whipped cream, in a leisurely way. At that time, it was real cream, neen o yer ersatz stuff. They stopped to watch. The boy was generous with the cream, and as he pressed down the top of each cookie the cream overflowed. Then he raised it to his lips and carefully licked off the surplus before laying it on the waiting tray.

Dothers were valuable property. Tam, a merchant in Ellon and a farmer as well, kent e richt side o a penny. He had four dothers, two of them married, another a teacher, and a fourth helping at home. When it happened that a farmer came to ask for the teacher's hand in marriage, Tam wisna neen pleased aboot it. 'Dyod', he said, 'it's a peety ye couldna see yer wye tae tak e ither een – I've a gye lot lyin on that een.'

Schoolteachers are well placed to get an insight into child psychology, and Mabel Smith's stories are often very revealing.

A Turriff lassie, Laura, had been visiting her mother more than once in Turriff Cottage Hospital when her baby brother was born. After one visit she met a neighbour and commented: 'They fairly get redd o the bairns at the Turra Hospital. Near aabody that comes in gangs awa hame wi een'.

Four-year-old Sammie wisna weel pleased fin a baby sister arrived. Next day he was up early and went outside. He met the neighbour, a carter, who was just setting off on his rounds. 'Wid ye gie's a horse for the bairn?' he asked.

Mr. Gordon was headmaster at Turriff Secondary School in the days when I was there myself. One day a parent asked his daughter, one of the newly-formed infant class: 'Fit hymn did ye sing e day?' Back came the answer: 'Gordon's always near us!'

At Milne's Institution, there was an Infant Mistress who had recently admitted quite a number of infants. For a simple lesson in counting, she said to them that she'd been for a walk in the fields and had seen many different kinds of animals. They had to count how many she had seen altogether. 'Fifty calves, 50 cows, 100 horses . . .' 'Oh', said a youngster new to the district, holding up his hand, 'that must hae been Orbliston. They say he has aye far ower mony horse.' And it was true that Mr Shepherd of Orbliston had a great name for horses.

The rector at Milne's Institution was Mr. Wishart. Once one of the junior staff was off duty and he had to look after the class. To keep them occupied, he got them to write out the Lord's prayer. One child began: 'Our Father Wishart in heaven . . .'

Since we're spikkin aboot bairns, here's story that wisna Mabel's style, bit I got it fae ma aal freen an former boss, David Murison, editor o *The Scottish National Dictionary*. It happent at a wee skweelie in Buchan, on the first day o a new intak. The bairns were in a line an e teacher wis gaan ben e line takkin a note o ilky een's name. She come till ae lad that widna speak, an wis like tae get roused wi im, till his neeper took peety on im an said, 'That's Geordie. Nivver min im. His auntie hid im till a sodger'.

David was always full of stories, especially ones that had a wee bit of value-added zest. Here's another sample. A wifie bade in a thackit hoosie wi a hingin lum. Ilky mornin she made er tae in a wee roon metal tae-pot, fullin't half fu o leaves and leavin't at the side o the peat fire aa day, jist toppin't up aye wi fresh water aifter she'd poored a cup. It got fine an black an strong. Ae day a young loon cam tae see er, and she asked if he'd like a cup. So she poored een oot, pittin in plenty o milk and sugar, bit he took ae sip an said, 'Oh, me, I canna drink it, it's ower strong!' 'Laddie', she said, 'fin I mak tae, I mak tae, an fin I mak water, I mak water.'

Mabel Smith was born in 1897, just over a century ago, and her father in 1875. They lived at Burnside, Ellon from 1899 to 1900, at Mains of Slains from 1900 to 1902, and then when the farmer moved to Leys of Auchmacoy they went with him and stayed there from 1902 to 1907. They were at the Home Farm, Auchmacoy from 1907 to 1909, and at the Home Farm, Philorth, from 1909 to 1915. Then they went to the Home Farm, Frendraught and stayed

from 1921 to 1932. Though this is a lot of moves, it is not as bad as
the six-monthly flitting of unmarried servants or the annual
flitting of married cottars. But Mabel, in telling her reminiscences,
many of them about these places, aye said it wis a lot o skirlin for
little oo.

At one farm where her faither got a temporary job as loon
because someone was ill, they got saps for supper gey aften. The
source o a lot o the loaf cam tae licht at a wintry time fin the roads
were blocked an e fairmer couldna visit his sister in Langside as
usual wi the pony an trap. He wid aye fess butter an eggs till er. So
he sent Tam e foreman on fit, cairryin a basket, for little fairm
work could be deen. On e wye hame e took a short cut by Ardlaw
Wid an ower e moss. He kent be the wecht that the basket wisna
teem, so he took a look. It wis full o crusts an aal loaf, fine for saps,
bit this time e birdies got it an naebody at e fairm asked fit happent
till e crusts.

At anither fairm, the mistress didna aften come intill e kitchen,
an Mary the deem wis aafa gweed tae the men. Bit ae day near
denner time, e mistress happent tae gang intill e milk-hoose an saa
a bowlie stannin full o thick cream. She speert fit it wis for an Mary
said it wis for e chappit tatties till e men's denner. Wi at, e mistress
poored e cream intill e ream jar, an skimmed aff some thinner
cream. 'Noo, slap em up wi at, Mary, at'll dee nicely.' Bit fin she
left, Mary jist reamed anither bowlfae, an iver aifter e men aye tellt
er tae slap em up wi that.

I suppose aafu fyow fowk speak o ream for cream nooadays, bit
e word wis still bein used in Mabel's time, though ye can see it wis
weerin oot, for it wis cream that cam oot o the ream jar.

Ae fairmer, wi a bit o a wint, had his sister as hoosekeeper. He
aye hid tae hae butcher meat till eez denner, bit though eez sister
aye let im ken in gweed time fan fresh meat wis nott, he didna aye
heed. In that case, she'd cook a hennie. This he nivver ate, jist

carved it up, an set it in its ashet on e fleer. Syne e'd yoke e shalt an set aff for e butcher's. The men got the hennie at supper time. This same sister wis the first Mabel's father ivver saa weerin troosers. They were her brither's. She put em on for e hoosework, for skirts, lang at that time, 'raised e styoo'. She wis baith a practical lass, as ye can see, an a diplomat, for er brither aye insisted on fresh-baked oatcakes for brakfist. Hooiver, his sister jist bakit twice a week, an on ither mornins jist heated some up on a bakin-toaster an e nivver kent e difference.

The diet wis sae scanty at some places that single men aften hid tae steal if they got a chance. Mabel's father didna set oot tae steal, bit if e cam across e nest o a hen that had laid awa he'd ate an egg, shell an aa, jist raa. Bit a lot o men stole hens an aa an cooked em in e chaamer.

Whiles it wis a hard life on e fairms, an it wis little winner that the men aften moved ivery sax months. If the grieve went, sae did aabody else, makking a clean toon o't. But as Mabel Smith said, conditions varied greatly. At one place her father was at, there wasn't even a chaamer. Him an anither man sleepit on a caaf bed on the fleer o e laft abeen e cairt shed, an of coorse there could be a gweed up-draacht atween e fleer boords. As it happened, the winter he spent there was one of the worst, thirteen weeks of snow and hard frost, an nae divaal. The two of them even kept a hammer at hand to knack their boots off the floor in the mornings. They took it in turns to buy a bottle of rum to keep themselves alive, so I doot a lot o their wages geed doon their thrapples. An little winner they wheekit an antrin eggie.

Hard times, right enough, yet on the occasions of weddings in the old days, they didna stint. Mabel's father told her that at a wedding they were at in the 1920s, a man sitting beside him asked:

'Div ye min on e weddins we eest tae be at, fin ye got near a hale hen tae yersel?' That was the time wedding feasts were held at home, not in hotels.

But these times were the exceptions, and there were always some folk worse off than others. When the Smiths were at Philorth, there was an under-keeper that lived on the 'bents', where it was just about impossible to make a garden to grow the usual tatties, kail and cabbage. This lad was a Highlandman and one day when Mabel's father was newsin with him, he learned that the pay was very poor too. 'But', said the keeper, 'ye jist need to be findin things.'

Mabel thought that a lot of folk must have been hungry at the beginning of the century. She was told that when she was little, she used to pinch any food that was left where she could see it, 'for fear it wid gang wrang'. And she would get up in her sleep, walk to the foot of the bed, and make as if she was nabbing something and eating it, then smack her lips and go back and lie down again, still sound asleep. Nobody ever seemed to think that she was maybe hungry.

So Mabel, like a lot of young folk, feeling 'spring hunger', a longing for green things in the spring, would eat sooricks, either single leaves or leaves put neatly one on top of the other to form a pad, which they called a loaf. Besides that, they ate yellow primroses and wild violets, sucked the honey from the wild clover flowers, and peeled the bulby bits of the flowers of the Scotch thistle, which they called cheese. They also ate the young beech leaves and the soft parts of grasses, and any wild fruits they came upon.

Then there's the way folk behave towards food in the North-East. Ye hidna tae be ower greedy. Mabel's grand-uncle Alick was apt to say it was nonsense to eat when you weren't hungry, but once he was hungry and had to keep from eating, through the force of politeness. He'd been invited out to his tea and seeing that he lived on his own, he'd gone ready to enjoy a good tuck-in. 'Bit', said he, 'they aa began yon "No thank you" caper till I wis the only een left eatin', and he had to no-thank-you himself out of his full supper.

Mabel spoke a lot about her folk. She'd been told that her Smith grandmother, when living at Lintmill Croft, went barfit in the summer time, which no doubt saved boot leather. Another economic tippie – which I've done myself in Auchterless – was that she sheared the grass at the roadsides to give to the cow. And it's true enough that many a crofter's cow was herded on the roadside, which was called the 'lang park'.

Since Mabel's grandfather was a semi-invalid, and the family was large, as was common at the time, life couldn't have been very easy. It had been the habit that a married son lived on the croft and helped at home. So her grandfather as the only son in the family began his married life at the croft. The Lintmill, where there had been a mill for processing flax (lint), was on the Pitfour Estate, and it was rented, as most estate placies were till after World War I, at least, and her grandfather being the oldest tenant by that time was allowed to end his days there without buying the croft.

This is an example of a good relationship between laird and tenant, though some tenants may have been better favoured than others. If the laird and his family were on a shoot in the area, they always asked to be allowed to have a meal at Lintmill. Bit this wis nae bother, or nae much, for they brought everything they needed with them. It jist meant giein em the best room, tables an cheers, an a big redd-up aforehan an a clean-up aifter. Work enyeuch, bit nae doot a big event in the lives of the Smiths, seein sae mony grand folks an their servants.

As Mabel remembers her grandfather, he spent a few hours every day in summer herding the cows by the Ugie, where the naiter girs grew lush. No doubt that was why the cream and butter and cheese tasted so fine and were in great demand in Longside.

There, one day, Mabel and a cousin noticed an old man sitting on a grassy bank, and taking off a boot and stocking. There was a hole in the toe. He took a bit o binder twine oot o eez pooch and tied it roon e hole, tae keep his tae fae bein hanged.

Her grandfather told her about an ailing cow one winter. It was wasting away, with no appetite, in spite of anything the vet could suggest. One day her grandfather decided to let her out for a change. She made straacht for a wee heapie o neeps an startit tae ate a rotten een. She improved every day ahin at. He said he'd heard of rotten neeps as a cure but had forgotten about it, and anyway he'd never tried it. But it seemed that animals could often find a cure for their own ailments if left to themselves.

One day there were visitors at 'Linties', and one was sayin foo rare e gairdens were at Pitfour and at Aden an so on. Fin they left, the aal man said tae Mabel, as serious as onything, 'I niver saa onything mair winnerfae than the flooers on the boortree'. At the foot of the garden, where the old mill had been, much lower than the road, boortrees had sprung up and the tops of the trees were on a level with anyone leaning on the barred fence by the roadside. This gave a great chance to enjoy the perfection of every floret, not to mention the lovely scent of the flowers – which I always thought was like champagne. Mabel said she thought her grandfather would be considered a failure by present standards – 'but we'd be none the worse of having more of such philosophers'.

Music was a serious need in the countryside before the days of the wireless and television. The accordion, the melodeon, the fiddle, the jew's harp or trump and even the spoons were common instruments and singing was also frequent on the list of entertainments. Mabel Smith's grandfather, when he was young, went to a singing class in Mintlaw that somebody had started up and carried on with a lot of success. Mabel remembers being sent to the attic one evening for an exercise book where he had written down the names of the folk who had joined the class and had also copied out the words and music of the songs they had learned. This set him off, and he sang some of the songs and told the history of many of the boys. His sisters had all learned to play the piano – which seemed to have been the thing for the lasses to learn – and so music must have played a big part in their lives. But her father was the only one in the family who seemed to have any interest in music.

Her grandfather wis a hardy character. He thocht naething o walkin miles. In middle age he'd walk fae Lintmill aa the wye tae Aiberdeen an back, on the same day, settin aff early and comin hame late. On a Sunday aifterneen, aifter bein at e kirk at Longside in e foreneen, if een o his sons wis fee'd a fair bittie awa he'd gang half roads tae meet im wi his clean claes an fess hame the foul eens, baith in a chackie. Div ye ken fit that is? It's jist a pilla case, originally made of 'chack', a cross-lined fabric, with a tape to shut it at the top. I kent it fine in Auchterless, and I've even photographed a farm servant carrying one. An faither an son an the twa chackies wid sit by the roadside an hae a pow-wow afore they geed their separate wyes again.

Besides roadside encoonters, there were twa places near Lintmill that were regular meetin pints, the smiddy an the souter's. Mabel's grandfather often went to the smiddy as a boy and chappit to the smith, that is he helped to hammer the hot iron on the anvil. It often happened that men brought things that needed repair to the smiddy in the evenings, so as nae tae brak e neesht day's yokin. There wis nivver a wird aboot overtime then.

It was the same with the souter, and the tailor, who would willingly sit up all night doing a job that was needed in a hurry. Once Mabel's father asked the Longside tailor to make a jacket for him. The tailor, being asthmatic and often not being able to sleep in bed, said he'd make it there and then if her father would stay up and keep him company.

Most working men with families had to do a bit of soutering themselves. They kept tinnies with sprigs for the soles of light boots, tackets for working boots, and had heel rings, toecaps, protectors of different shapes that you fitted together like a jigsaw puzzle, and a foot made of iron and fixed into a log of wood that you gripped between your knees as you hammered in the needful. There was also a tin with pointed bits of matchsticks. They were used to plug the holes if tackets fell out, before they were hammered in again.

Anither thing deen at hame wis barberin. The men geed een anither a crop wi a sheers or clippers. Boys often got a 'bowl crop', the bowl being laid on the head and the surplus scissored away from round about. And in ony case 'there's only a week atween a bad an a gweed crop'!

One thing Mabel's father remembered was the night of the Tay Bridge disaster in 1879, so her stories go back over 100 years. He was four-and-a-half years old at the time. Bit it wisna the Bridge that worried im, it wis mair the fact that the thackit reef o the craft hoose they bade in wis blaan aff. There he lay in his bed, lookin up at e stars, till the neebours cam aroon and helpit tae pit the reef back on, wechtin't doon as best they could till they could see better fit they were deein in daylicht. I'm nae sure foo they got on wi the thack, for I some doot it wid hae got a gey dirdin. Ahin at, Mabel's father wis niver aafa happy if a gale wis blaain.

One of the jobs her father did was to go the round of other crofters if their pig was to be killed. There was no question of using the killing house at the time, but there was a mannie in the district that specialised in the job; he was the pig killer for them all. But it needed all hands, and when the pig had been killed, and the bristles scraped off, it was cut up and there was a share-out all round. Mabel didn't know how it was decided who would get which part, though the main bits would have gone to the pig's owner. Every bit was used, naething wastit. The bacon was cured at home, and mealy and black puddings were made. Mabel's father had to help to fill the puddings. I've seen the neck and shoulders cut off a bottle that was used for this job, as a filler.

Fowk were gey hardy then. They were eesed tae liftin things tee. Mabel's grandmither, tae gie an example, got up at 5 o'clock an helpit wi the milkin three times a day till she wis over 70. As she got aaler, though, she didna like booin doon, so eence she askit Mabel an a cousin o hers tae weed the borders roon e hoose. She feesh a peat-backet tae haad e weeds. Mabel wis maybe 20 at e time an er cousin a fyow ear aaler. Aifter a file, they thocht they'd better teem e backet, bit they'd stappit it weel an werena fit tae meeve't. By comes grandmither tae see foo they were gettin on, she wis fair pleased wi the rate o progress, an jist pickit up the backet tae tak it awa, nae thinkin the ithers hidna been fit for't.

Water for the house was carried in frachts, i.e. two pailfuls at a time. Some folk would use a yoke across their shoulders, or sometimes just a wooden ring that you stepped into to keep the pails away from you a bit as you carried them. In the kitchen there was a recess in the wall (or it could be at the side of the entrance passage too) where the water pails stood, with a laving pan handy in one of them, and an enamel jug on a nail above. Mabel's grand-father often took a drink there and would turn to the rest and say: 'Yer stamach needs a wash as weel's yer face, ye ken'. They were well off for water, for there were three wells, two down the garden and one by the roadside. Here, a tin was always left, much used by passing pedestrians and by cyclists who had to come off anyway before tackling the steep brae. There were also various barrels and half-barrels round the house and an old bit of the steading to catch rain water, which was nice and soft for washing clothes.

Mabel's grandfather had a plain diet, but it had its highlights too. According to Mabel, his breakfast never varied: at 6 o'clock in the morning, a boiled egg, oatcakes and tea. Bit in the middle o the mornin he aye likit a moofae fae the whisky bottle. Aa the same, there wis an aafa lot o things he niver tastit. Denner wis at 11 o'clock, an he'd be ready for't aifter his early start. It was often cold silverside of beef, spread with mustard and eaten with oatcakes. His supper was oatcakes and black coffee.

The weemin fowk werena big eaters an they seemed tae enjoy their tea best o aa. This was teen at aboot half five (which everybody in the North-East knows is half-past four). They ate egg or cheese or caal chucken or various kins o fish. It's interesting that the men did not eat at the same time, but at 6 o'clock when they came in. They got the same things to eat, though. Cheese wis aye on e table. An they were surely aa feert o being late, for the kitchen clock wis kept a quarter o an oor ahead o the richt time – this wis a caper o ma ain mither tee in later days.

The women and the visitors – including Mabel when she was

there – always had something to eat and drink at bedtime. This is what we used to call our 'bed piece'. They all prepared what they preferred: some made stoorum, a tablespoonful of meal, with cinnamon and warmed milk, others had cold or warmed milk, or milk straight from the cow after it had been put through the search (the sieve – we called it the sye-er), along with one of Sandy Patterson's butter fardens.

Grannie and aunts were good cooks though they believed in good plain nourishing food and 'neen o yer doctor's drogs'. For dinner they had soups of various kinds made from beef-bree, broth, pea-soup, rice soup with chicken, hare soup to which they added curry (no doubt having studied the recipe books), potato soup and milk soups that were favoured by an uncle; then there could be stovies, stewed rabbits, fresh or salt herring with tatties and maybe a sauce; and there followed a milk pudding with jam and cream. If it was a milk soup day, this was usually followed by stewed rhubarb, often made into a pink jelly by adding tapioca, or other stewed fruit, or a dumpling if the weather was cold. And every day there were boiled tatties, except with milk soup. You could have them or not in your soup, just as you pleased. They had a bit of meat on Sundays. An surely they didna need milk and breid tae finish wi!

This was at Lintmill, and as far as Mabel could remember, her parents had only one weekend off in the year. This was a Saturday, Sunday and Monday, 'atween e hey an e hairst'. When they went to Lintmill, the two uncles and their family, who lived near, also foregathered and they had a latish dinner followed by tea and cake. First they had cold fowl, and it took a few to go round as there were thirteen youngsters from three families plus ten grown-ups. They sat ben the hoose, in the biggest but not the best room. This had once been the shop when the Lintmill had prospered. And it was full of odd recesses and corner cupboards and places that were handy for stacking dishes. After the meat and vegetables came a choice of puddings and then the tea and cakes if there was room left. Mabel and her sister got to stay on for the rest of the week when they were old enough, and that was their special holiday.

At Brownhill in Auchterless, it used to be the custom for the family to take their meals in a ben-the-hoose room, and the men ate in the kitchen. But in Mabel Smith's day, there were no ben-the-hoose meals. Her uncle at Lintmill o Hythie had all his meals in the kitchen, along with the loon, who slept in the house. Aabody ate in the kitchen

After dinner – which was in the middle of the day – Mabel's uncle and the loon had a flap in the barn among the straw, her grandparents and aunts had a nap in their chairs, and the young folk slipped ben-the-hoose on bad days or lay down on the brae face in the garden on sunny days. Apparently this was where her great-grandfather used to snooze too, lying on his face – which should have given him a crick in the neck, according to the physiotherapists, bit fowk dinna aye gang be the rules. He keepit a lot o bees in skeps alang the heid o the gairden, and ae day as he wis sleepin a skep swarmed an the bees lichtit on the back o his weskit. Naebody else at hame kent aboot bees an they hid tae get a neeper tae tryst e swarm awa.

On wet Sundays the two young sisters went up the stair to what had been the drawing room that had been turned into a box room. They'd get old dresses and bonnets out of a wardrobe and kist and put them on, great fun for the quines. Then they'd go down and visit the big fowk, and persuade their grannie to show them her collection of shawls and mutches, her wedding gown and trinkets, and they would as often as not end up with a sing-song of favourite hymns until teatime. Whiles even their grandfather was persuaded to show them the fancy waistcoats he used to wear.

In this way they got a lot of family history, but there were also more practical lessons to be learned. On wet days during the week, for example, they would go to the barn and help their uncle and the loon to twine hay-rapes with a thraahyeuk. The lasses twined and the men fed to them, for it was a skilled job to 'let oot' so that the rope would be smooth and even.

The buzzin o the bees lichtin on grandfather's back in the gairden min's me on the berry bushes there. There were plenty o them, so a lot o jam was made. As a matter of fact, the bulk of it was rhubarb jam, used at dinnertime on milk puddings, as well as at teatime. Bilin aifter bilin wis poored intil a muckle crock aboot three feet high. Eence Mabel wis asked tae clean a basketfu o goosers for makin jam. She began tae winner if she should pick aff the flooer or leave it on. So she asked her grandfaither. 'Weel', he said, 'if it's for yer Auntie Helen, pick it aff. If it's for yer Auntie Fanny, leave't on.' So much for diplomacy. Blackcurrant drink and raspberry vinegar were made if the crops were good, or if someone in Longside sent over a basketful. Mabel's grannie had a sweet tooth and liked to sup a bowlful of the hot jam – but she preferred syrup on her piece. There's no accounting for tastes.

Pots were scoured with sand till they shone like stainless steel, and made a bonny display ranged on the slats below a huge dresser, whose top was used as a workbench, and at the back there was a row of upturned bowls. An whiles forced cleanin wis nott. A pot bilin ower could mak some mess. A clood o saft ess wid rise an coat aathing aroon, nae forgettin e mantelpiece, and e fire micht even be drooned oot. So the secret wis tae keep the lids on pots raised a wee bittie.

When I was wandering around the North-East I saw a lot of old-style fireplaces. There were hingin lums, set against a gable wall, some of them with wooden sides – like at Mr Jeffrey's house at Ardoyne, near Insch – and once when I paid a visit these had just been removed because they had nearly taken fire. Bit eence the timmer had got a gweed scam an wis weel blackened neesht e fire an aa charcoaly it was maistly safe enyeuch.

Open fires like that were open to the sky at the top, where the outlet was like a wooden box often tied around with rapes. On coorse, weet days, sitty draps wid come doon, so it wisna jist gweed for ony bakin that wis goin on. Bit Mabel Smith's grandparents had a cure for that. They had made a recess alangside e main fireplace, some like e set-up for a wash-hoose biler, wi a fireplace an a great big girdle biggit in abeen't. So it wisna jist anaith e draps, an I'm sure that it wid bleck ony architect tae ken fit wye there wis a double fireplace in that hoose, if they were tae be lookin at it nooadays. Hooiver, it wis jist a practical idea, an it worked.

All the ironwork was made by the local smith, including the big semi-circular oatcake toaster that sat on the hearth of the main fireplace, where nothing but peats were burned. Mabel thinks that some coal could be added to the baking fire, though. The smith also made a brander for fish, in the shape of a girdle but with open zig-zag bars, and there was an iron contraption like a pair o tyangs with flat legs, meant to raise the lid of the hens' pot. The hens' pot wis biled in e aifterneen, syne it wis chappit wi e tattie chapper an left tae sit by the fireside so that it wisna caal in the mornin. Nae saat wis used, bit tatties, neeps an ony orrals were biled, syne sids or oatmeal or Indian corn were chappit in. I've chappit mony a hens' pot masel at Pitglassie, an boy! fit a fine yoam it hid. Ye nearly grudged it till e hens.

Mabel's grandfather as a young man had been six feet tall, but a 'healthy' open air life with continual soakings had left him with rheumatism and asthma. By the time she remembered him, he had become so hollow-chested and bent that he looked quite small. When walking he used a stick, a rung of a stick off a tree with a good handhold but without a curved top. The fireside I've mentioned was his special corner, and, except on special occasions, he took all his meals there, because it was too uncomfortable for him to reach up to an ordinary table. He had long white hair and a beard. He lived till he was 89 and could read the papers without glasses, though he had suffered from cataracts on both eyes. Apparently the doctor had put drops in them and fluid oozed out of them for days, but in the hinner end he got his sight back.

Her grandmother never had a doctor and a dentist was never near her teeth. She did the job herself if a tooth had to come out, using a big strong pair of scissors as a lever, and applying a hot peat from the fire from time to time as a painkiller. Mabel's father had seen her at it, though she didn't know how the peat was chosen or how it was held. At least there were always bits of dry, hot, black peat on the outer rim of the fire.

Grannie was only once in a train, from Longside to Peterhead and back again. As she said, she hidna nearly lang enyeuch o't!

Mabel's Aunt Fanny was a great one for cures, if you would call them that, or at least she wis aye ready wi wise advice in times of illness. She had a kind of roving and enquiring spirit. She never stayed long in one job but she gathered up information wherever she went and was in great demand for looking after the sick. Jist e kinno buddy ye nott in e days afore e welfare state!

Mabel's father said that when she had a half-day off when he was still a youngster, she would come back with a parcel of steak. For tea, she wid wallop this wi the breid roller, neen o yer fancy tenderisers, and grill it over a red fire. This was said to be for the good health of their father and an invalid sister Helen, bit I'm sure it widda been a great treat for aabody.

If anybody brought a present of something eatable, like fancy biscuits – an ye wid niver pey a visit withoot something in yer han – Aunt Fanny, in her later years, was all for laying it by for visitors, but Aunt Helen wid hae neen o't. She said that if visitors werena pleased wi fit they got there, they'd jist need to bring their ain mait wi em. Helen was quite right – most visitors were very well pleased with good country butter, eggs, cheese and cream, or fish if the fishwife had been, and they wouldn't have looked at fancy biscuits (or so Mabel thought – bit I doot a hungry loon widda been myangin for e biscuits tee. And in any case her grandmother loved good chocolates and could never admire enough the skill of the toon-folk that made them).

Once, at Frendraught in the 1920s, two men came to put sheep on the neeps. There was chappit tatties for the dinner and the men were hospitably invited to join in. The family was surprised when both of them flattened their tatties with their spoons and then spread syrup over them. So iver aifter they pulled their father's leg, tellin im that wis jist fit wis nott tae gar the tatties slide doon. But he never tried this improvement.

There's differences in taste and differences in the ways of making things in different parts of the country. One of the Smiths' neighbours was from Perthshire. When she made oat-cakes, they were a good half-inch thick, and not as big as the local ones. She made them in the forenoon and fired them in the afternoon, because they were too soft to handle straight away. Mabel never saw her baking but she saw the pile of uncooked oatcakes on a corner of the table, one above the other, maybe a dozen, waiting for the late firing. As they stood, the meal would swell and the round would become firm. This is very different from the thin quarters of oatcakes that were the North-East standard. Women in Aberdeenshire used to vie with each other aboot foo mony cakes o breid they could pit oot in an oor. Of course, families went through a lot of oatcakes in a week. They were eaten with tattie soup and with milk soup, and with stovies, which didna aye slide doon and you had to drink a mouthful of milk now and again. An jist anither thing aboot bakin. If scones were on the go, you couldn't slide them onto the girdle as you can with oatcakes. So you folded each scone as it was shaped in two, then folded it again, and carried it in your hand to the girdle. There you laid it on the right spot and opened it out, patting out any creases. When you were learning you were apt to make holes or tear away a bit of the round. If the fire was too fierce you just hooked the girdle up by the crook on the links of the swey. There's skills in aathing!

Aabody seems tae hae plenty o aathing nooadays, bit in e aal days ye hid tae mak dee wi fit ye hid. So I thocht I wid tell ye some o the tippies on domestic economy that Mabel Smith hid heard o.

Until World War II you could get white flour bags for next to nothing. They had to be washed to get the flour out of them, and then boiled and bleached until the red and blue lettering on them had disappeared. Then they were used in place of cotton for linings, for bandages to keep cheeses in shape in the chessel, for dish towels and even to make chemises. There were different qualities and some of them were quite fine. Bit like aathing else, the bags got far ower dear and the eese o them stopped. That's progress!

If you were in need of a new spurtle for stirring your pots, you made it out of a worn sweeping brush handle. Spurtles aye got shorter as they were used, and had to be replaced, like aathing else. It's a funny thing, bit I aye kent it as a spurkle, and according to the *Scottish National Dictionary*, the pronunciation with –k- is fairly standard for the North-East. The word comes from Latin 'spatula', the same as the doctor haads yer tongue doon wi files fin he wints tae see intill the back o yer thrapple.

In winter time, the creesh – grease – from a fowl was put in an old cup, and left beside the fire to keep it liquid. Then it was spread on boots with a piece of old cotton tae haad oot e snaa bree. In fact, one of Mabel Smith's aunts liked creeshy hens for making broth, rather than chickens. Sheep's heid broth made a cheap dinner if you liked mutton, though this was not usually fancied in the North-East. A cousin had told Mabel that West country people loved mutton broth swimming in fat. But fat on soup was liked in the North-East too, though not mutton fat, and soup 'wi nae an e'e on't' was considered a sign of meanness.

If you were baking scones or pancakes, you had to grease the girdle. This was done by putting suet into a piece of cotton, tying it at the neck, and then rubbing it on as the girdle stood over the fire, so that the heat melted the fat. This was the suet clootie. But it was never used for oatcakes. Another hame-made invention was a bunch of stiff turkey or hen's feathers, used to brush the loose meal off a baking board before the round of oatcakes was slid on to the girdle. It was said that some weemen could turn a cake o breid on the bakin-boord by tossing it up like a pancake, but mostly it was done by laying a second board on top and then turning. That was less skeely bit less chancie.

The fye – whey – from cheese making had a lot of uses. It was held to be a healthy drink. When Mabel's parents were young, in the second half of the nineteenth century, fye-brose was among the many kinds of brose made. The system was that the whey was boiled and the top, called the 'fleetins', was skimmed off to make the brose. It seems that fleetins is a word only found in the North-East. But Mabel's method or memory may not have been accurate, because a source of 1923, *Swatches o' Hamespun*, speaks of 'fleeten brose', and says that 'meal wis pitten intill sweet fye, an' the scum 'at raise wis skimmed aff, an' that wis aften oor supper'.

When the Smith family was at Mains of Slains in 1900–1902, just at the turn of the century, many of the local men, if they didn't go to the church on Sunday morning, would converge on the braes at Old Slains Castle for a news in fine weather. There was maybe mair sociability tae life then. Mabel remembered going once with her father, who had probably taken her along to see the yellow primroses that formed a perfect carpet.

At Mains of Slains, the road to the farm ran through a field and the gate to it was at the foot of their garden. The bold Mabel, at the age of three or four, would run to open the gate to save anyone getting down from a passing cart or a gig – which they called a 'machine' – and then close it again. A rare wee jobbie! She got a good impression of the transport of the time. She had a photo-graphic image in her head of two particular occasions that must have impressed her. One was when she let a governess cart through. A lady was seated on the left, a bearded gentleman on the right, both neatly dressed in black. The lady spoke to the young lass and smilingly asked her companion for a penny to pass over. The second time she wasn't opening the gate but noting from the window a great steam-engine hauling a threshing mill and fixed behind that a muckle grey van where the mill men slept if need be. As it passed there came a great rummle of thunder and her mother, who was terrified of it, cried suddenly 'That's lichtnin', and Mabel, not at all scared, took it that 'lichtnin' was the name of the never-before-seen apparition that had just gone by.

Bicycles were fairly common by the beginning of the century, and several of Mabel's female relatives had them, finding them a great help in getting about. She had a story about two of the men at Leys of Auchmacoy who were going to Aberdeen for a day, catching the early train at Ellon a few miles away. But they slept in and one of the bykes had a burst on the way. Still, they managed. The foreman cycled a bit, then left the byke and started running. The second horseman then took over and bykit on a bittie, syne ran. Nae doot they got gey hait, bit they made it.

The doctor was one of the first to get a motor byke and when it went along the road they all turned out to watch it.

The girls wore boots, not shoes, at that time, with metal protectors on the soles, toe-pieces and heel rings. They liked to scuff their feet in the dust of the Aberdeen to Peterhead road. They would also wear gaiters fastened by buttons at the sides, using button hooks. In winter, nearly all the girls at Artrochie School wore them. In Mabel's parents' time, buttoned boots were fashionable best wear for ladies, often with beautiful buttons – and every household had a button bag for old buttons cut off old items of clothing, kept to do a second turn.

At the sides of the roads here and there would be a heap of stones for road metal, and a stone-knapper wearing goggles to protect his eyes would gradually turn this into a neatly shaped bing ready for measuring, because he was paid by the amount done, and then it served for repairing the road. One of Mabel's uncles thought it would be better than farm work and tried it, but it was a monotonous job and he soon tired of it. It was mostly older men who broke stones.

It seems to me that winters were stormier a wee filie back than they are noo. Mabel Smith tellt some stories about snaavy wither tee. There wisna aye roadmen handy tae shovel snaa, and since there wisna much chance o ootdoor work, fairmers wid set their men tae clear the roads wi shovels or hame-made widden snaa ploos. Before this, they would probably air their horses by taking them along the roads. Several pairs going and coming would beat down the snow a lot, but then if it froze it was just about impossible to walk on the many horseshoe marks without skidding or hurting your feet. When taxes went up and more roadmen began to be taken on in the early 1900s, the farmers stopped sending men to help except in emergencies.

At the doors of the farmhouses there were usually scrapers tae get rid o the worst o the muck on yer beets or sheen afore ye steppit intae the hoose. The smith at Auchmacoy made a very neat one for the family. It was sunk into a stone, and had two curly 'horns' at the sides, and two hearts on the blade for decoration. Whenever the family flitted it went with them, and it lasted for over fifty years. But often just any old bit of an implement would be hammered into the ground to make a scraper. The Smiths' scraper, though, was held in high honour, and on special occasions it ws cleaned and polished up to high doh like the fireside, using blacklead. There were special blacklead brushes, with a curved wooden back and a tufty at each end for getting into awkward corners. Blaik was used for cleaning boots, and originally it came in cakes made up like chocolate. You had to melt it with water, which was a messy job, and as Mabel said, it was loathe to shine. Later it came in more manageable tins.

Visiting relations still goes on, but it used to be very much a part of everyday life. Mabel and her sister were often sent to visit an aunt and uncle with three boys roughly of the same age, and visits would be returned. The two younger boys used to try to frighten the girls by telling them they would die on a certain day if they ate such and such a thing, usually something growing wild. As they walked on the way, they would be wary of passing houses with a dog, but folk often invited them in and gave them milk and pancakes. If it was a Sunday, their parents might collect them. There were three single men at Leys o Auchmacoy, so Mabel's father was toondie every fourth Sunday, and was free on the other three except when there was an emergency. Of coorse there wis a lot o newsin and they'd be late in getting back.

But discipline was strict at home and the girls were never allowed to wander. When the cousins came they got more freedom to roam the fields and corners of the woods, looking for nests, frogs and toads, and digging for lucy arnuts. If they found a foggy bees' byke they would burn the moss and grass around to be able to steal the honey.

In earlier days in Buchan, there seems to have been much more visiting of relations and several of Mabel's stories throw light on such occasions. Sometimes they would visit an aunt who was a maid with the Arbuthnots in Peterhead, or else they went there so that mother could visit the dentist. To get there they took a train from Auchmacoy to Boddam and finished the journey by bus. This was a great event for the quines, and there were plenty of passengers. But there was no heating system on the train in those days, though in winter time a metal container maybe 3 feet long by 9 inches by 4 inches, filled with boiling water, would be pushed into the carriage at some station, and the cold one removed. You could heat your feet on this.

Mabel's favourite visits were to a grand uncle and grand aunt who lived at a place called Braeside. This was a thackit hoosie, standing in waste ground where there flourished funs and breem, birk busses and rodden saplings and wild flowers galore. Her grand uncle was a roadman. They had a family of six sons and two daughters. All began work as farm servants, and the eldest became a roadman, two joined the army and were killed in World War I, three joined the Liverpool Police Force, and the youngest learned to be a gardener. It is interesting that they did not want to stay in farm work. They got tired of constant hard work and poor wages. Many young lads emigrated to Canada but if they married young they tended to stay. According to Mabel, it wasn't actually farm work that was disliked but the way many had to slave in all weathers, which crippled many a one, and then you were looked down on if you could't do your stint. An uncle of hers was heard to say it was no pleasure being a foreman if your health broke down. And then there were the challenges, to see who could last out longest in a heavy job, maybe cairryin hivvy bags o corn up e stairs intil e laft, an beatin e foreman at it.

Maybe the weemin folk had mair sense. Still, they had their own rivalries. They were very keen on pot plants on their window sills, especially fuchsias and geraniums. Ma ain mither wis the same. And since there was a big pot of geraniums on the sill near the end of the table where I sat in the evenings, I was very familiar with the scent, which makes me think of dead flies because there were always some on the rim of the plate that the pot stood in. Windows were often small but no one seems to think that the plants kept out more light, and some had even pots half way up the window as well. You were one up if you had a hanging pot plant. There were special outer pots with three chains on a ring for hanging plants like columbine, links-o-love, Jerusalem honeysuckle and so on.

Mabel's grand aunt hid an aafa bonny gairden, wi fine coloured flooers in the borders. There were dusty millers, pansies, carnations, roses, yellow marigolds with black centres, mignonette, tam thooms, balm and southernwood, each with their own scent. Honeysuckle and roses – they had scents too at that time! – rambled over the walls. There were vegetables and fruit bushes, and strawberries, and even if the sons did some of the spade work, it was her grand aunt who was fond of all things growing. In the kitchen she was just as painstaking at cooking the simplest dish and adding little extras to taste them. But her two daughters were not too fit. Both were consumptive, and though the older one was cured, the other died in her early twenties. And grand aunt had her treasures too in the house. She would sometimes take them out to show Mabel, and she would get presents – a length of delicate lace, a ribbon, a particularly pretty Christmas card she had kept, and all with a lingering scent. Little wonder Mabel enjoyed her visits.

When Mabel was little, her mother's mother lived at a small farm on the Hill of Dudwick. On Sundays there were always crowds of visitors so that tea – that means supper, ye ken – had to be taken in relays. There wid aye be somebody that took an interest in the youngsters, giein them fruit an flooers fae the gairden or takin them for a walk tae the aal quarry hole. Folk were great walkers at that time. One of her mother's cousins would walk all the way from Methlick, for they liked to be there in the cheery company and on sunny days there was a fine sheltered bank where they could sit, enjoying the open air.

Mains o Dudwick ran the local Flower Show. The Smiths would go to it, because the mistress of the house had been Mabel's mother's aunt, a great entertainer in her time. Foo did she get tae be mistress? Weel, fin she wis bidin at the Hill, an was free, the fairmer at the Mains had written her a notie tae speer if she'd be hoosekeeper till im. She wrote back sayin she widna, bit she'd come as his wife. So he agreed. I doot it widda been a Leap Ear!

However, visiting was mostly done by relatives, which kept up the closeness of family ties. And if a visit was paid, it had to be returned. A grand uncle's wife was very particular about exchanges. She lived in the Slains district and later moved to Tillery, to a dairy farm. At that time, dairy farming was gey hard work, for ye'd tae be up at 3 o' clock in the mornin, tae dee the han-milkin. Pails o milk were heavy an had tae be cairriet till the cooler, an ye hid tae hae plenty o hait watter tae plot aa the utensils, an aye the same again in the aifterneen. But the returns were good, so anything not connected with dairying tended to be neglected. They shouldna haen much time for visitors, bit there wis aye plenty o them, for the hoose was on the main road till Aiberdeen, an aabody wis made welcome. For the bairns there was a grand swing in the barn, an they never got tired of it.

Mabel has a fine story about this great aunt. She was built on a grand scale and had a loud voice and a commanding way with her that used to terrify Mabel's sister. Once when Mabel was there, as a student on holiday, a grandchild of 6 or 7 was there at the same time. The dother o the hoose, in the neest room, loot an almighty sneeze, garrin Mabel jump. The grandchild wisna impressed. She said 'Granny can dee't far better than at'.

There were two uncles, single men, who always turned up at the term times. They always brought sweets – jujubes, Scotch mixture, conversation lozenges, Cupid's whispers – that the quines never got at home. Aunties and cousins would come as well, bringing other presents – a birthday box, a needlecase, a thimble, a big coloured glass bool, a bottle of scent such as Jockey Club, which they thought was somebody's name so the stress went on the word 'Club'. The men wid smoke their clay cutties, and the melodeon wid get goin, an singin an recitin, wi a lot o fun an jokes afore tea wis made. Bit the quines thocht they were hard deen till. In the day-time they were sent oot tae play, in the evenin they were pit tae their beds, though they could aye hear the on-go. An they werena allooed tae spik unless they were spoken till. But Mabel had an answer for that. She would just speak to the palin posts, turning ilky een intill a different buddy.

About the turn of the last century there was plenty o entertainment. Nearly every farm-servant could play the melodeon and plenty could play the fiddle. Mabel Smith had a memory of a dance at Mains o Slains when she was about three years old, that she thinks was at the time of a meal-an-ale at the eyn o hairst. A meal-an-ale was held when the last of the stalks, the clyack shafe, had been cut and carried intae the hoose to be hung up for giein the beasts in the byre and stable a tooshtie at the New Ear, or else it wis fin aa the crap had been taen in an the fairmer hid got winter. The pairty wid finish wi the dish o meal-an-ale, made wi oatmeal, ale, sugar and a gweed drappie o fusky. Often a ring was put in the mixture and aabody raxed in wi their speen hopin tae be the lucky finder, for they wid be first tae be mairriet. In Kincardineshire an a bittie farrer sooth the clyack supper wid be the 'maiden feast', and across the boddim o Scotland it wis the 'kirn', bit the fine meal-an-ale mixter wis a pure North-East invention, it seems.

Feein markets were great sources of entertainment, and even into the 1930s they were thronged. You could hardly force your way along the main streets in towns. And there was always Rascal Friday in Aberdeen the week before the term, for the folk that still hadn't managed to get a fee.

Mabel's unmarried grand uncle told her that when he was young he wouldn't go to school. But he regretted it later. At his first placie, he was in a chaamer with a much older man, and this lad could read, and often read the newspapers and books aloud for the loon's benefit. So, says he, 'I begood to see at I wis a muckle feel', and his friend taught him to read and to play the fiddle. He became a crack hand at fiddling, and was in great demand at weddings, dances or just for an evening's pleasure. When at his own home, the Hill, he'd be going home when other folk were getting up and he'd hear somebody saying, 'At's at neer-dae-weel devil o a fiddler jist awa hame'. Bit he didna smoke or drink. Aa the same he wisna aafa fond o work, an he'd jist work enough tae live on for a filie, used it up, then had tae work again. He went to America for a time, bit jist did the same there. He didn't go to make his fortune.

A certain amount of entertainment came from wanderin-aboot fowk. When Mabel was young, there were a lot o tramps, though they were a bit o a terror tae folk livin in oot o the wye places. Some of them were old soldiers. One of their favourites was Danny, who wore moleskin trousers, washed till in the distance they looked white, so you could spot him from a distance. Her mother usually bought small things from him, pairs o pints, buttons or thread, and she would give him a piece to help him on his way. He would say 'Ta ta, good bye and thank ye'. Maybe more tramps came around than usual, because a neighbouring farmer, Tammy Gairdner, would give them a meal, and a night's lodging in the barn. It was the same at her Smith grandparents' place, for they would ask in certain of the tramps and give them a big bowlful of soup or a cup of tea with something to eat. In return they got a lot o news and aften a good bargain. Bit Mabel's mither couldna unnerstan this, likely because she wis gey aften her leen in e hoose.

There wis a Flower Show at Auchmacoy, held in a tent in the grounds o Auchmacoy House. Of coorse, it wisna jist flooers an vegetables, bit ye could get prizes for knittin, better kent as wyvin, needlework, bakin an so on. There wis open sports as weel, an if I'd been there I widda tried for the jumpin an the fit races, for I wis aye rale gweed at them an I wis hardly ivver beaten in the mile. It's a rare feelin tae be fit an rinnin free, jist as gin ye wis floatin. Onywye, at the Flooer Show there wis a dancin boord tee, for baith young an grown-up competitors. For fun, there could be a hat-trimmin competition for the men, ilky een gettin a lady's aald strae hat an some odds an ends for trimmin. On the ither han, there wis maybe a nail-drivin competition for the ladies, each getting a squaar o 1-inch thick wid, a certain number o brass-heeded nails an a haimmer. They hid tae knock them in in the shape, say, o the big letter 'R'. The men wid pit their hats on for the judgin an of coorse there wis plenty o laachin. Ye could get tea in a tent, bit the local fowk maistly geed hame for their tea an come back for the dance in the evenin. A great day oot, I wyte!

Bit human naiter bein fit it is, there were wyes o 'enhancin performance', as they say aboot the druggie boys at the Olympics, an Mabel geed some examples. Ae wifie wis geen a length o flannin tae mak a pair o draaers for a bairn, bit she jist cut a hole in the middle tae let in the bairn's heid. She happent tae win the prize for button-holes, so the whisper geed aboot – 'bit of coorse she hid a son at wis a tylor'. A mannie that hidna a decent carrot in his yaird managed tae win the prize for carrots, an somebody tried tae pass aff a heed o Sweet Williams neatly made up be tyin on some extra sprigs. Bit the judge wisna sae blate – he jist chucked it anaith e stagin. The challenge could bring oot the worst in fowk, an surely it made for excitement, for weeks afore e Show the men wid be gaan the roons inspectin een anither's gairdens an weighin up their chances o a prize.

Aikey Fair wis anither great day, in the simmer. It wis a recognised local holiday, an it wis still a horse fair when Mabel was at Philorth, though fin I tried it masel nae that lang syne it wis jist a fun fair wi chair-o-planes and stands o aa kins bit nivver the horse tae be seen. Mabel min's that the manager at Philorth aye geed till't, an in the hoose they hid a postcard o the Fair, jist a sea o horses, an the manager there in the foregrun. She wis nivver at it hersel, bit a cousin o hers widna miss it, for it was there she met mony freens an acquaintances an got aa the news. Bit it's aye the same at Turra or Keith Shows, I doot.

Eence fin Mabel wis at her grandfather's, she wis invited till a Church Guild Picnic. They went tae Pitfour in a charabanc, bit in earlier days they widda traivelled in cairts, steeped in the dam an scrubbed for the occasion, an the horse harness polished tae high doh and decorated wi rosettes. Ither wyes o traivellin wis in a brake, wi seats up ilky lang side, pulled be ae horse (the charabanc had fower), in a spring cairt, a square box wi a seat across that could be pulled forrit or back dependin on the load tae be cairried, or in a landau, wi padded seats across an biggit in. This wis favoured be aaler fowk because it wis low an easy tae get intill.

When Mabel was at Mains o Slains, she was sent to the Sunday School, though she was only four years old. She remembered nothing about it except that they gave her a wee card with a coloured flower at one corner, and a text that she had to repeat on the following Sunday. It wis maybe enyeuch tae pit onybody aff, bit onywye, it's aa she could min' aboot it. Her early memories were maistly short flashes, though when school began, she could full the story oot mair.

There were drill lessons at her first school, at Artrochie. The girls began. Each of them got a wooden hoop, as they took their place a certain distance apart on the floor in rows. They were told the movements they had to make, then the maister played a tune on the fiddle in waltz time and they had to keep time. When the boys' turn came they had to perform with dumbbells.

If the headmaster came into the classroom in the morning wearing a woolly gravat, the class knew there would be trouble. He would start with Bible, and when the class showed its abysmal ignorance, the peer man would lose his temper and out would come the strap, for he knew that the inspectors, when they came round, were keen on that subject. This was in the early years of the twentieth century. So he would set them some written work an there widna be a soun, bit fit they didna realise was that he had a cold and was just trying to save his voice.

Classes II to VI would work together for drill, singing and Bible. Sometimes, one class had to come to the floor to do sums when the maister was busy with another class, and then they had to stand in pairs, back-to-back, so that they couldna copy. The bairns were never called by their Christian names. Mabel was Miss Smith, Senior, and her sister, Miss Smith, Junior.

When she first went to school, they didn't have Christmas holidays. They had a day off at the New Year, a Term Holiday, a week at the end of May when many of the cottar folk were flitting, and there was the Hairst Play, six weeks at harvest time, when the bigger pupils had to give a hand in the fields.

Sometimes there were entertainments at the school. There was once a magic lantern show, and the bairns' fowk were there as well and there was tea and buns. The bairns had to bring their own mugs and the boys soon emptied theirs and got on wi the fine job o blaain up an burstin the bags. They once went to the sands at Cruden Bay for a school picnic, travelling along wi the big fowk in the train. They waved an shoutit tae ony body or beast they happened tae pass, an the fowk waved back an the horses boltit an capered. There were aa kin's o races an they had a lot o fun, and enjoyed getting their prizes.

Then there was prize-giving day at school. Prizes were presented by the minister. Mabel got *The Babes in the Wood*, and her sister,

117

The Sleeping Beauty, both with big print and fine coloured pictures. But the minister and the schoolmaster fell out and the prize-giving afternoons came to an end.

Once an inspector turned up on Shrove Tuesday. First he examined the big eyn, then he and the headmaster came through to the little eyn, which was presided over by a young lady teacher. While they were busy, a boy got the chalk and wrote on the blackboard:

> Beef brose an sauty bannocks
> Lat's hame to full wir stamachs.

The inspector wisna a north man, and he was a bittie puzzled an amused, bit aa the same the school got a half-day. It wisna till the Smith family were at Philorth that they had beef brose just to see what it tasted like, and it was just grand. Father had eaten it before but not mother, who didn't like brose. So it looks as if the custom of eating beef brose on Fastern's Een had just about died out by their time.

There was a School Concert organised at Artrochie School, with performances for two nights running. But it says something about the state of transport in the earlier 1900s that some of the parents refused to let their bairns turn out the second night because of the distances they had to travel. The parents went with them once, but could hardly be expected to come a second time.

Bit there wis ither concerts in e skweel for e big fowk. Mabel geed eence an it wis fair an eye-opener, for the room wis crammed till e windae-sills. She wis amazed at e fowk she aye thocht hid been timmer-teened (it's a grand word that, timber-tuned) that were stannin up tae sing, an example bein the son o ae fairmer, supposed nae tae be very bricht, dressed in aal patched duds, an aal felt hat an a reed gravat, roarin oot 'Robin Tamson's Smiddy' an getting encore aifter encore. Sad to say, one young lass, the best actress, had a long way to cycle home, and after being overheated in the crowded room, she caught pneumonia and didn't recover. This ended the interest in concerts, and in any case events connected with the School were not often repeated.

The bairns were never kept off school for bad weather. Once when they were at Philorth, there had been a severe snowstorm. On the Monday the snow was feet deep, and it was freezing hard when they left home. Their father told them to go by the Big Hoose, which wasn't allowed as a rule but he knew nobody would be going out that day. By cutting past the North Lodge they would get to the main road, instead of using their usual way by the Links. The main road would be easier if there had happened to be any traffic. When they got to the School their faces were in a halo of frozen breath, and there was no heating, for the pipes had burst. But they went to their classrooms and carried on as usual, and every half-hour or so they were told to gather in the main hall and were made to race around for ten minutes or so to warm themselves up. Nobody would volunteer to play the piano to make things cheerier, and little wonder! By the afternoon there was a little heat and pupils from outlying districts had arrived. The amount of snow was unusual for a seaside town and it lay in heaps at the street sides for weeks. For years after, you could buy postcards of a Fraserburgh street in the great storm.

The best schoolday of the year was the day the school closed for the Hairst Play, when they had 'Sax weeks tae tear wir claes, an ae day tae men em'. This 'one day' was the Monday off. On this last day, they buskit the school. Leafy branches were carried in and stuck in the slots in the desks that usually held the slates. Incidentally, cloots were kept tae clean e slates o the marks o skylies. Ye jist hid tae spit an rub, an the loons wid use the sleeve o their jaiket tae gie a final polish. The cloots seen began tae smell.

No real lessons were done on that last day and the class was free to chatter, until some wicked boy would make a smart remark and the master would give him a reprimand, which would surprise the bairns because they thought they were well hidden behind the greenery. Of course, they couldn't disguise their voices. Bit e tag didna come oot that day, for the maister wis nae doot in high gweed humour at the thocht o his ain sax weeks o freedom. They were let out early, though the boys had to clear out all the branches first. Buskin came to an end like other old customs. For one thing, the school-cleaner objected to the mess made by the leaves. But until Mabel told me about buskin, I had never heard of it, and there's nae a word aboot it in the *Scottish National Dictionary*, though it's seldom that David Murison missed onything. So there's anither item for the record o Buchan words.

Fin caal nichts is comin, ye maybe begin tae winner fit fowk did for coats in the aal days. In the early 1900s, Mabel Smith's faither didna possess a coat, bit she min's on bein teen till Aiberdeen wi im tae buy a hivvy overcoat. Till then, he had only a grand Inverness cape that he put on when going for the milk on stormy nights. The fact is that workin men didna wear overcoats. Their jaikets an their breeks had tae be weather-resistant if nae water-proof. They didna aften wear a jaiket, even, bit sometimes a sleevet weskit, the material o the sleeves nae bein as hivvy as the front. I've heard this kind of waistcoat being called a shafter, because it had two 'shafts', or sleeves. In simmer, some wore a kin o smock made o a strong cotton material. This was maybe like what John Smith, Mabel's father, told me was a corseckie. It was worn in a lot of the farming districts of Scotland, not only the North-East, and was sometimes made of striped cloth. The origin of the name is not very certain, but it's like an old Dutch word, *kasack* or *kasacke*, 'a cloak, linen garment, worn by men or women'. I've just seen one example, but it was a very practical thing, because for dusty jobs, you could fix it tightly at the neck, sleeves and waist, tae keep e styoo oot.

As far as the bairns were concerned, toys – at least bought ones – were practically unknown. When the Smiths were at Mains of Slains, the farmer's widowed daughter, who acted as housekeeper, gave Mabel a marvellously dressed wax doll, but her sister managed to smash it, and so, for comfort, somebody gave her a stick doll, though that wisna jist the same. It was a wooden doll with a brightly painted face, and for long after, when she saw a woman with red cheeks, she wid min on e timmer dallie. It was easy to make a doll out of a sock. You just flyped it (turned it outside in), and turned it round so that the heel represented the doll's face, then tied a cloth or shawl round it and laid it in an old box.

Mabel got another disappointment when Geordie Forrest, the merchant in Collieston, gave her a ring. She wore't aa the wye hame, bit there she took it aff an let it faa. It rolled ower the widden fleer o the closet and disappeared doon a moose hole. In cottar houses, the closet was the spacie between the kitchen and the 'room'. The parents slept in a box bed in the kitchen, that jutted back into the closet. The two girls slept in the recess made by the side of the box bed and the wall of the closet. Visitors got an iron bedstead, with brass knobs, in the 'room'. There was no bathroom. In fact it was a world's wonder when they were at Artrochie School, for two new cottar houses were built at Artrochie Farm, with bathrooms. This was on Auchmacoy Estate, when the laird was Miss Buchan.

Bairns have wonderful imaginations. They can get fair lost in their play, making worlds that big folk have forgotten. Mabel and

121

her sister played at hoosies with broken crockery, 'lames', and also at shoppies, with little stones for money, sand for sugar, docken seeds for mince, scraped neeps for butter. Even bits of coloured paper were precious. An example was the wrapping of 'Pinkie', pink stuff used for cleaning spoons, shiny and with a peculiar smell. They also played at schoolies, and of course every bairn wanted to be the teacher and get to use the strap.

And Mabel played too well at schoolies, for she went on to become a teacher herself.

FIVE

Willie Mathieson's Notebooks

I came across a very interesting notebook in Edinburgh. It had been written by Willie Mathieson, Castleton Cottage, King Edward, and sent to Professor Angus McIntosh at The Linguistic Survey of Scotland. This was in 1952.

The notebook is a miscellaneous collection of words and phrases, place names and stories, and I'd like tae gie ye some samples. It's jist amazin foo much knowledge aabody his in their heids, if they'd only let it oot.

Willie mentions 'yirlin a yellow bird, gorbelt young ones, fykie tae blaw means you cannot blow them when the young ones are in the eggs'. This brought me back to my young days, when, like every other boy, I looked for birds' nests tae herrie and picked out an egg to blow to keep for my collection. As a matter of fact, I still have the collection, in a glass-topped display box that came from my father's old shop in Pitglassie – he used to have shoelaces an sic-like in't for sale. The yirlin, or often the yalla-yirlin, is the yellowhammer, but in Auchterless, jist tae be different fae Kinedart, we caaed it a yalla-yitie or a yaldie-yite. Bonnie wee birds they are, bit the loons had a coorse rhyme:

> A yaldie-yite,
> Sat doon tae shite,
> At the back o a marble steen.

It's actually the eggs that are gorblet, before the young ones hatch out. After that they are gorblins, when they sit in their nests an if ye pit yer finger in they aa open their beaks like pairs o shovels, lookin for mait.

Willie Mathieson also mentioned 'win casen a tree thrown by the wind, Larick larch . . . rosit The sticky substance from the Larch or fir trees'. Win casen, wind cast, speaks for itself, a fine descriptive expression. Rosit is resin, and though on the trunks of the trees where it oozes out it is gey clairty stuff, in its more commercial, harder forms it was used by souters on their threid for makkin rositty eyns, and by fiddlers for their bows. Some o the loons wid tak e rosit aff e laricks an chaa't like chaddy, an maybe it wis gweed for e teeth, bit I canna say I ivver tried it masel. The bark of the larch, when it was covered with moss, was called foggy-larick, and sure's death, e loons, aye up tae aa e tricks, wid try tae smoke it like tobacca. The name of the tree has a funny origin. It was introduced to Scotland about the 1700s and then spread. It didn't have a Scots name, so the Latin name was used, 'Larix', which sounded like a plural 'larick-s', so the single tree became the larick.

Like all country folk, Willie Mathieson had a lot of weather lore. 'A bad sign is to see the moon lying on her back with the old one in her arms is a sure sign of a gale or bad weather . . . And also the weather gaugh or gall (gaw) when it's a long time good weather Bad weather is sure to follow Another sign of bad weather is the stars shooting across the sky'. Sometimes a wither-gaa is a special appearance in the sky, like a mock sun, or a bit of a rainbow, which I knew as a 'teeth' (a 'tooth' of a rainbow, but with the usual North-East change of -oo- to -ee-), but as Willie said, it could be a fine spell too, usually sandwiched in between two periods of bad weather. It was thought that snow would follow it.

Willie was obviously a good hand with a horse. Of yoking a young one he said: 'Many a time I've seen them, oh ay an been at the job too. It's whiles a job getting them to pull you know and that's when a lot of people thinks you are bad using them. The best thing ever I used was kindness I just used to go in about and say well lassie or laddie, whatever it was. I'd only one young horse . . . I used to come in aboot and say well beastie are you ready to pull come awa than and try a wee bittie and strange to say they very often came with a clap and a cuddle. And I aye found kindness was best'.

Then he went on to speak about the 'mert'. 'When I was young they used to kill a pig or a fat stot. If you killed a stot this winter I killed a pig the next then everyone for a few miles roon . . . got a share of the mert as much as be a dinner for the good part of the winter. You steepit it amongst brine and boiled so much then sometimes you would get cold meat for dinner. I'll be making your teeth water for you winna get that nooadays not even get leave to kill them now let alone get a bit cold meat.'

Weel, aabody kens fit a stot is – it's jist a young bullock – bit maybe the custom o haein a mert or a mart is farrer awa noo fae e memory o maist fowk. The mart was a well-known custom in much of Scotland by the fourteenth century, and was often one of the items included in payments of rent, as well as money. In earlier days, before fridges had come in, fresh meat didn't keep very long and it had to be salted in barrels. This meant that everybody had a lot of salt (in saat fish an saat butter tee), but only from time to time, because meat wisna aften to be got in the daily diet. Sometimes ither craiters were dried and salted for the winter, bit they were maybe lookit doon on a bittie, because there's a story that goat's flesh wis kent as the 'poor man's mart'.

There wis a bit o celebratin at the time the mert was killed, with fresh meat, and some sharing of fine bitties with the neighbours. But besides this there was the winter supper, held after all the corn was in the corn yard and the rucks aa thackit and trimmed and the tatties all up and pitted . . . The farmer would then say come boys and get your winter supper for ye deserve it. It was a substantial feast, beef broth, boiled or roasted fowl, potatoes, sweets and plum duff then well washed doon with home brewed ale and a liberal supply of whisky then they had tea but instead of milk they put whisky which was called the birse cup then for a game of cards or as the old farmer said, we'll hae a game at the deil's books.

'Deil's books' is not a specially North-East phrase, but a standard English expression for playing cards. If they didna play cards they wid try the totum, a square-sided spinning top with letters on each of its four sides: T stood for tak een, D meant dossie doon een, N was nickle naething and A was taks aa. The stakes were pins or pennies, or bigger amounts if folk were in the gambling mood. This is a very old game, known in Scotland from about the year 1500, and you might say it has classical origins for the word totum is the Latin word that means 'whole'.

It's interestin the wye oatmeal and milk products were important pairts o sic customs. Since we're jist past the tail o the ear, I'll mention a custom wi sowens. I've spoken o them afore, bit here's Willie's story: 'there is no word o eel (Yule) noo a days, there was sowens made you see and you were invited here and there to your sowens'. He explained how sowens were made from sids, the husks of oatmeal. 'They were put in a bowie and left for three days to steep then on the fourth day you put them through a search or strainer to drain every drop of water which was white and left nothing but the husks, then they were mixed with treacle or syrup (i.e. the liquid) and made into drinking sowens or made like porridge. I liked the drinking sowens but not the supping, there was some farmers made porridge and gave you raw sowens instead of milk but thank goodness I never got that'.

Aal Eel was on 5 January, and after that first came Candlemas and syne e new meen, and the first Tuesday after that wis aye Fastern's Een. And that was beef brose an sauty bannock day. But with Willie there was more sport. Then the boys would get hold of a long rope and fix a hook at the end of it, and go fishing down the lum. They would try to catch the handle of the girdle with the bannocks baking on it, but the exercise was never very successful because the rantle tree across the chimney – a bar of wood or iron for the crook and the links – would not let the girdle past. But as Willie said, 'it was sport seeing the wifie in a rage as her bannocks disappeared up the lum, we would be fined for the half that we did at that time I can tell you but that days are gone'.

Weel, here's anither o his stories, this time tae dee wi local history. He spoke about the Cockerty Stones on the Hill o Auchmaleddie in the parish of New Deer. Now, 'cockerty' is an interesting word, meaning rocky, unsteady, and if somebody had not been well and was getting about for the first time, ye micht see im cockerin aboot e close. These stones were big ones, of quartz, that were resting on top of other ones in such a way that the slightest touch would make them move, but as the years went on they got bedded into the ground and the movement stopped. 'Auld Nick was blamed for carrying them there in his apron but the string broke.' Fit Aal Nick wid hae tae dee in the North-East, I dinna ken, an fit he wid be weerin an apron for I dinna ken either, bit that's the story.

Thinkin o the deil made Willie min on stories aboot ministers. 'About that time the public houses was open on Sunday, and the elders and a good few of the congregation got half seas over. An elder in the parish of New Deer was once asked if he ever saw his minister drunk. 'Na, na', he said, 'ony time I wis haein a dram wi the minister lang afore he was half slokit I wis blin foo masel, man.'

One Sunday this same minister was about to announce the psalm to be sung when a man stood up and said, 'I say, minister, ye'll pray for ma mither'. 'Wha's your mither?' 'Tam Stott's mither.' 'Whaur dwalls she?' 'In the parish o Shivas in the lands o Touxhill.'

Here's a gweed bit o reportit speech fae Willie's pen: 'Man, Geordie Christie is tae get mairriet', 'na I didna ken that, fa is he takin it's likely an oman body', 'o it's an oman body aa richt it's Christina Moffat her that's been hoosekeeper at the Mains for an aafu length o time, I thocht Mains imsel wid a hid some say bit Geordie's bate im', 'a weel, weel, he winna hae his sorras tae seek puir sowl, she's an aafy spendthrift'. 'Weel I dinna ken, I heard she was mean and Mains eence said she was the greediest person in aa Buchan, her sheaves o loaf she cut ye could read the Lord's Prayer through them'. 'Ha, ha, that may be, bit Mains hid maybe kent it gey weel afore e lookit through it.'

Here's a story fin Willie wis a loon at hame: 'We wis in the moss ae day, the old boy an me, fin an auld man cam ower tae hae a news o my father. You see he wis only new into his placie at May and of course I'd never seen him afore, he'd an awfu dronin wey o speakin and he says, "Dod, Willie, I cam awa ower tae see if you would cast my peats, man you see I'm only new in an I hiv aa the neeps tae pit in so I wis winnerin if ye'd cast mine". "Oh weel", the old boy says, "ye'll hae tae winner for I'm castin nae mair the year, you can gang doon tae this man at the fit o the moss here." The mannie didna wait nae langer he gaed awa.'

128

One of the jobs that Willie's father did on wet days was to make besoms. Besoms were made from heather or broom or hair and were of various sizes for different purposes, whether sweeping the church or the passage an the greep in the byre, or dichtin the hearth stone. If yer hoose wis besom-clean, that meant it wisna very tidy, for you'd swypit e fleer bit left e styoo on e furniture an hidna washed e fleer.

Willie was a good hand with the scythe, and he knew about sharpening it with a 'broad'. This is a flat wooden board like a little bat, with a handle at one end and a covering of sandstone or a kind of carborundum mixture at the other. The earliest date I've found for the broad is 1882 in Banffshire. The name 'scythe-straik' or 'straik' was also used. In the more southerly parts of Scotland another style of wooden contraption was actually fixed at the upper end of the handle of the straight-handled scythe that was common in the area (but hardly known in the North-East); to use it, it was taken off its clip and fine sand was sprinkled onto it after a layer of tallow had been spread on, and this is maybe the origin of the broad that plenty of folk will remember in the North-East. Another interesting thing is that in Perthshire in the 1840s trunks of oak trees were found in peat bogs that were being cleared, and it was said that the country folk split them and sold them at markets as straiks for sharpening scythes. Of course it was only in the early 1800s that the scythe began to replace the heuk for cutting crops of corn, to any great extent, and there would have been a greater need for straiks or scythe steens or sharpin steens after that. But the blades of scythes from Roman times that have also been found in Scotland were sharpened by laying the blade on a little portable metal anvil with a spike that you stuck into the ground, and tapping the edge with a hammer.

I some doot if ye're wirkin a scythe naebody wid be able tae blame ye for idleseat.

There was an old shepherd used to visit Willie Mathieson's father, an took a likin tae the loon. So Willie had some stories about him, an here's a sample: 'It was that same shepherd that I once saw sitting crosslegged on the top of a gate post playing the chanter or I should say learning to play, he got on like this "wi my hey din dirnie hey din dirnie hae" then he tried the chanter then he would say "Na, that's nae richt, wi ma hey din dirnie how din dirnie hey din dirnie hae", and I stood an watched him for a good while an aye efter that he thocht a lot o me, of coorse, aa tinks likes ither. "Ay, ay, loon", he wid say, "ye widna like tae be a shepherd wid ye? Man, it's a fine job, mind of course ye're oot in aa kin o weather ye ken, that's jist the warst o't for a beginner and that jist finishes it" '.

This made Willie think o ither stories aboot wither: 'I mind on a Ellon Market a fairmer he cam in aboot to fee a lad and they stood an argued a guid file and the fairmer says "weel, are ye takin the shillin?", meaning the arles. "Weel", the lad says, "I'll come tae ye on one condition that's if ye dinna wirk on coorse weather". "O weel", the fairmer says, "we dinna lowse for a shooer and a steady rain wi never hae" '.

This gies ye a gweed idea o the kin o dibber-dabberin that geed on at feein markets. There was a bit of fun, and no doubt the stories improved with telling, but the basic theme is the greed of the farmer and the efforts of the folk looking for fees to do a little better. And loons were certainly 'exploited', to use today's politically correct word. On one occasion, a farmer asked Willie's father if he could come to build some dykes to see if he could get the beasts kept in. ' "Ye're a gran han at it, you can tak the loon wi you if you like it will be aye something to him." I gaed wi him aa richt but I never saw nothing for it. That same fairmer ance asked me tae come an help store neeps an I said "Na, I got naething for the dykes". "Oh my goodness, laddie, I gave it to your fadder to give you." "Oh well", I says, "I hinna got naething yet." "Oh weel, laddie, if that's the state o maitters come ye an help me store neeps and I'll see you get your money this time." So I went an I pooed and tailed and topped 2 acre of swedes and was paid 7/6 the acre for it, bit I jist took a piece wi me an in tillt again sae ae day I wis going on and Mrs Forbes the fairmer's wife says "Lord, come into the kitchen an get a bite o meat, min, ye'll need tae mind it's the belly that keeps up the back", so I wis forced tae gang wi the wifie and there wis three women washen oot the fleer so she jist fell tee with her pail an a cloot, I wis a kind of feart I wid be washen oot tae. The wifie says "dinna work sae hard min, cause a willin horse aye gets mair a dae nor ane that's nae willin tae work"'.

That's a fine example o a fairmer's wife takin peety on e loon.

Willie didna hae a great opinion o Rhynie fowk. He said there were some differences in the speech, and one of his examples was the 'fleed for the end of a field Top and Bottom'. Well, I've heard the word masel fae aal fairmers in Auchterless, so maybe it wisna jist Rhynie, though 'eynrigs' cam tae be fully mair common. At ony rate, it's only in the North-East that ye get 'fleeds'.

According to Willie, the differences in speech had been levelled out to some extent because 'a lot o Buchan hummlies went up there fairmers and fairm workers because the folk up there aa wore top coats at their wark you see, so there is nae sae much difference in their speech as there was when I went up there. Man when I was up there you would been better to have had four spare watches for it was aye the say afore ye wis lang yokit, fit time is't? Oh me me, first sax o clock an my supper that's aa they lookit for I got fed up I made on I wis awfy deaf an didna hear them or else say ach I'm nae gaun tae wear doon ma watch tae please you, na na, you'll need to buy one yourself or you'll soon hae my one done'. Aa the same, Willie was the man with the watch!

Willie had a fine example o neeperin. 'Hiv ye hear o auld Tawse?' 'Na, fat aboot im?' 'He's lost his coo, min, ay wi the milk fivver.' He gaed ower tae a neeper fairmer an he says 'Hiv ye a coo to sell by ony chance?' So the fairmer says 'ay, I've twa, come on oot tae the byre an see them'. So the fairmer says 'tak yer pick, this een here her time is oot [her calf is due] so ye winna hae lang tae wait for milk. Bit this ither een her time is nae up for three weeks yet'. 'Ah, dod, bit', says Tawse, 'I wid hae likit ane to gie milk jist noo ye ken.' 'Ach, weel, I'm sorry bit I canna help ye wi that, I'm afraid, ye'll hae tae try some ither body.' So puir auld Tawse didna buy the coo, he wanted one a lang lang time till they gaithered up for one and gave it to him. So he landed on his feet.

SIX

Snippets Fae Ither Fowk

One of the pleasures of doing a monthly piece in the *Leopard* is the number of folk who write to say how much their memories have been stimulated, an fit's mair, they aye add a snippetie till e store o knowledge aboot e North-East. So I'm gaan tae gie credit faar credit's due, leave ma notebooks aleen, an gie ye an inklin o fit ither fowk hiv been tellin's.

Charles Allan, Montrose, wis on aboot sowens. As the son of a miller and farmer, at Kinrake Mills – the biggest country mill in its day north of Edinburgh – they regularly had sowens at the old home in the evenings when they had come home from school and lessons had been done. This was always drinking sowens. His mother, brought up as a girl in Montrose, used to tell them that she remembered well a wifie who came round the doors in the town with big flagons of sowens for sale, crying out as she jogged along, 'Suppin sowens!', or 'Drinkin sowens!'. This must have been a bit like the selling of soor dook from the carts that used to come round, at least in the towns farrer sooth. They didn't use a sowens sieve at Kinrake, like the one I told you about from the farm of Brownhill, but just a bit of muslin or fine cloth of some kind for sieving.

Some of you will likely min on Charles Allan. He was one of the advisers at the Agricultural College and started in 1925 (when he wrote me in April '94 he was 91), as personal assistant to

G. G. Esslemont, and attended William Findlay's lectures in applied agricultural botany at Marischal College. Findlay was another miller's son. Charles Allan went on to be adviser in Shetland, then Orkney and Ross-shire, then back to Aberdeenshire including Cruden Bay where William Findlay's old mill was. It was said by the old folk around that William ran the mill himself, and after he had set the 'beas' mait', in the mill, he would take his book fae e crap o e wa and get on with his studies. That is surely how lads o pairts are made. He would bicycle into Aberdeen to the College for a Botany class at 9am, whiles.

Bit that wisna e only letter aboot sowens. I had another from an Ellon quine, Mrs Margaret Stuart (née Johnson), now living at Methven, Perthshire (an surely hyne fae hame). I'll tell ye the story jist as she geed it till's:

'Fifty ears ago, Great Auntie Lizzie and my Grannie sat at the fire and suppit their sowens. I hid ae taste and that wis eneuch. Lizzie started tae lauch and syne telt this tale.

Fifty ears afore, she wis coortin Great Uncle Jim. Lizzie hid a curfew time and, on the chap o ten, she wid enter the hoose and bang the back door shut.

"Fine", thocht her folk. "That's Lizzie safely in."

But Lizzie wis not in. She wis on the idder side o the door makin her way in the dark tae far Jim wis waitin in their favourite trystin place – the wash hoose.

Something wis wrang.

"Jim", whispered Lizzie. "Faar are ye? Ye muckle gype, fit hiv ye deen?"

"I'm aafa sorry", said the drippin figure. "I trippit ower something and fell into the bath o sowens." '

They baith hid some explainin tae dee and efter that the wash hoose wis oot o boonds. I some doot that's an example o sowens wi some body in't! But joking apart, it's from such stories that you learn about the old days, and from this one we can learn that part of the preparation of sowens was to let the sids settle in a bath in the washhouse outside. Like feel Jock, we're aye learnin.

Jamie Morrison, at Wallace Road, Inverurie got in touch wi's a filie back. It was a tremendous pleasure to get his letters, because they proved to me once again – nae that I nott muckle convincin – that there is a great encyclopedia of knowledge out there, just waiting to be opened. So we'll jist turn a page or twa an tak a teetie.

In a letter of 31 October 1995, Jamie told me about the aal thackit hooses. The couples were jist smaa trees split in half an held at the tap wi timmer pegs. Then they were covered with a layer of what looked like branches, about one to two inches in diameter, and the layer of divots went over that. The divots were what his grandfather called heathery divots. They were cassen be the flachter spaad where the heather was short, about two to three inches deep, and they were laid heather side down on the roof.

Then Jamie told about the covering of breem – and this is information I haven't seen anywhere else. You had to look for young breem busses, about fifteen inches long, and they were cut with a heuk, which left the ends pointed. The broom was put up into sheaves and stooked up for a month to six weeks tilll it was wun, and then it was ready for use. When a hill was cleared of old broom bushes, using an iron breem dog, in a couple of years after that it would be covered with young bushes an gin they were four to five ear aal they were ready for cutting. So you can see that in the old days a broom hill was not just a bonny sight of yellow flowers and black, crackling pods in due season, and a haven for birds and wee beasties, but it was also part of the everyday working system as an important resource for human comfort.

The next stage in rethatching was that a ladder was put up the length of the roof, and with a trowel the aal thack wis scrapit aff e divots over a space about a foot wide. Starting at the bottom, the new broom was pushed into the divots and bunches were laid one over the other all the way up. The finished roof would have been about six inches deep in new broom. It took Jamie's grandfather about a week to finish a house.

Then to secure the roof a wire was drawn tight along the whole length, set about six inches up from the bottom and pinned down by timmer pegs that were driven into the divots. That was all that was needed to hold the roof, and it was fairly wind and water tight. As Jamie said, 'a new thacked reef looked bonnie'. I can only agree with him, though I have never seen a breem thackit hoose myself, but only one newly thatched with straw and clay once at Cranloch, Lhanbryde in Moray, and that was certainly a fine sight. It was done by Mr Brockie.

Clay was also used in the broom thatching technique. Clay mud was mixed into a paste and spread along the top of the roof where it grew as hard as cement and never needed to be replaced – which is likely more than could be said for cement.

As Jamie said, 'Please yersel aboot the letter, Div ye think it worth? Awfu pleased to help ye, to me it just seems like yesterday'. Aye, information like this is aye weel worth.

Jamie Morrison had a grand memory! As a laddie he would do things with his grandfather and got the job of working the gaad when they were scything. This meant using a stick or wand to make sure the stalks of corn lay right onto the scythe blade, and Jamie wis aye telt tae keep a step in front and watch the pint o the scythe. This jist soons like common sense, bit as ma aal skweel-maister eest tae say, common sense is uncommon sense, an I doot there hid been a fyow mishanters at the job, itherwise grandfather widna hae bothert tae pint oot e need for care.

Syne there were wis fit e caad 'storm stooks'. His grandfather always put up the stooks in such a way that there were four sheaves, one at each corner, 'wi a tit o corn tied roon the tap'. They were much better at standing the wind and were hardly ever blown down. But that was just done on the crofts. Bigger places didn't take time to make storm stooks.

This is a very interesting survival of an old technique that was widespread in Scotland and further afield in earlier times. The name for this kind of stook was a gait or gaitin, a word that goes back to the seventeenth century. Often the sheaves were set up in ones, with their bottoms well spread out and with the bands tied near the tops. This helped the drying in damp weather, and it was said that the corn was less likely to grow in the sheaf. In North Tyrone in Ulster, 'goats' were set up in fours, just like on Jamie's grandfather's croft, and the *Scottish National Dictionary* has a report dated 1928 from an Aberdeenshire informant of hay sheaves set up in threes: 'We were passing a hay field this summer when a man in my company said "Losh, man! it's lang since I've seen hey gytit". "What do you mean by 'gytit'?" I asked. "The shaives are set up in threes an' a raip is wuppit roon the taps tae haud them on faan".'

This would have been seed hay, and that's something else Jamie telt me aboot. On a small place the hay was cut with the scythe, 'and the sheaves were bun nearer the craps and the sheaf just douped down singly'. Jamie actually said also that this was called a 'gytin', giving what must have been the North-East pronunciation of the word. The way they used to thrash it for seed was to lay a ruck cover on the ground, put the sheaves on top an jist gie them a lick or twa wi the back o the graip. It fairly got maist o the seed oot.

It is remarkable how special needs sometimes preserve old practices. Once I was contacted by a big East Lothian farmer, in an area where you would expect all the most advanced farming techniques to be practised. He wanted to give some things for the Scottish Agricultural Museum at Ingliston, in the Royal Highland Showground. So I went out to visit him and, to my utter astonishment, he had a couple of flails in the barn, things I had never expected to see outside the smaller-scale farming areas. But these were of a special type. They had the usual wooden handstaffs, but the souples or beaters were made of rope, and were longer than the handstaffs themselves. They were intended for threshing seed hay, and this probably explained the use of the long rope souples, as well as the survival of the flails in the Lothians for such a specialist purpose. Some of you may have seen them when you've been down at the 'Highland Show'.

Files ye hear fae hyne awa, an I'm gaan tae tell ye fit a lad in Canada wrote, a North-East exile, Bob Little, MB ChB FRCS(C), in twa or three letters.

A while back, I'd spoken aboot neep brose, which was made with the bree of boiled neeps instead of boiling water, which, of course, gave them a special flavour. Bit tae haad the speen, ye hidna tae be ower genteel. Ye hid tae 'grip the thing in the kneive, speen side up, hannle doon'. It's a funny thing fashion, but there's ae thing sure, an that is that our ancestors went in for a lot of 'speen mait'. Aabody kens that the 'richt' wye tae sup yer broth is to tip the plate away from you, yet that's just fashion. On the fairms o the North-East, and in all the country districts, you tilted the plate towards yourself, as I did myself and still do to this day, more since I found that my friends in other European countries did the same. There's maybe mair chance o cowpin some on tae yersel if ye tip it till ye, bit there's nae doot it's the aalest and maist widespread style.

Syne Bob spak aboot skirlie. Here is his recipe: 'Mix in a bowlie new meal, ingins, a pucklie suet, saat and spice "to taste". Heat a skillet. Add fat, preferably bacon. When a hint o blue lowe is rising, teem the bowlie intilt. Steer. Turn doon the heat. Fin its a bonny gowd, bit afore it's brunt, nae ower greasy, bit like bunker sand in consistency, it's done'.

And then there was mealy puddin (which in Auchterless we always called 'mealy jimmies'). As a boy in the 1930s and '40s, Bob saw them made: 'Ingins and suet were sweated in a pan, then added to a pail of meal, until each grain of meal shared a little of the fat. Salt and pepper were added. I think the pail then sat overnight. Next day, endless casing was mounted on the spout of a special funnel, and the mixture was fed in from above. As the puddings emerged they were separated by double (paired) knots. The resultant string of puddens was then stored (as I recall) in a large pail, filled with dry meal and used with the traditional mince and tatties.' Bob is convinced that it was because of his skills learned tying mealies that he became a surgeon!

In another letter, February 1995, he tellt me a true story. Faiver heard o a gweed story at wisna true? His grannie at Newmachar had a croft and lots of pigs, and his father was a gardener. Grannie's neighbour had a big lorry and in 1940, when Bob was ten or eleven years old, they had loaded the lorry with dung and were headed for Aberdeen, but were stopped at the corner at Parkhill by a troop of sodgers and the local bobby. The bobby approached.

'There's a rumour aboot German spies . . . fit's in yer lorry?'

'A load o shite, ye damn feel'.

The bobby then grabbed a graip and stabbed the dung. He then pompously walked to the cab and asked, 'Noo, ye widna hae onything ablow that shite?'

'Aye, I wid.'

'Oh, noo fit wid that be?'

'Mair shite ye damn feel, noo get oot o my wye.'

Weel, maybe it's nae jist e politest o stories, bit I jist gee't as I got it.

And tae finish off, I'll jist mention that Bob was born in a house in Hilton Drive, Aberdeen in 1929, and was educated at Hilton Primary School, then at Robert Gordon's College, and at Aberdeen University, but maistly, he says, his real education was on his grannie's craft at Swailend, Newmachar. An he's niver lost his ain tongue.

Glossary

Aabody, everybody
aafa, terrible
allagrooze, grim, sour
anaith, underneath
antrin, occasional
arles, earnest money
at, that
atween, between
ba, ball
backet, wooden container
bad use, to ill use
baikie, tether pin
bailie, farm-servant in charge of
   the cows
bairn, child
bannock, pancake
barfit broth, broth made with a
   little butter, but no meat
barfit, barefoot
beel, fester
beelin, a festering sore
beet, boot
begood, began
ben-the-hoose, through the house,
   in the best room
besom, a broom, brush
besom-clean, moderately clean
big, build
bile, to boil
biler, boiler
bin, bind
bink, ledge at side of fire
birk, birch
birl, whirl

birse, bristle, used by shoemakers
   in sewing leather
bishop, to tamp down loose earth
   with a 'bishop'
bismer, 'steelyard', weighing
   machine in a corn loft
bizzie, stall floor
blaik, boot polish
blate, foolish
bleck, beat, confound
blin siv, a 'blind sieve', not pierced
   with holes
boddim, bottom
bondie, bonfire
boo, to bend
bool, marble
boons, bounds
boortree, elder tree
bout, row of cut corn
bow, a boll of meal, c.140lbs.
bowie, bowl, tub
bowsel, type of cattle binding
branner, brander
bree, liquid
breem, broom
breem-dog, iron lever for rooting
   up broom
breet, brute
breezle, hurry, rush
breid, oatcakes
breist-spad, a peat-spade, worked
   in from the face of the bank
brig, bridge
broad, scythe-sharpening board

141

brose, oatmeal dish made by
pouring boiling water on meal
brunt, burned
Buchan hummlie, a hornless
Aberdeen-Angus cattle beast
(here used figuratively of folk
from Buchan)
bun, bound
busk, to decorate
butter clappers, a pair of wooden
boards for working butter
buttermilk breid, thick, relatively
soft oatcakes
ca canny, be careful
caa oot, to drive out
caal, cold
caap, wooden bowl
caddled, of eggs, scrambled
caff, chaff
calfie's cheese, beestings
carvy, carraway
cassen, cast, dug
cassie steen, cobblestone
ca-throwe, drive, energy
chaamer, outside accommodation
for single farm-servants getting
meals in kitchen
chackie, linen bag for carrying
dirty washing
chaddy, chewing gum
chap, to mash, to hammer
cheer, chair
chessel, chisel, cheese-vat
chiel, 'chap'
chout, creature (sarcastic)
claa, to scratch
claams, clamp, for holding leather
in flat stitching
claik, a gossip
clairt, to spread

clairty, sticky
clappers, for butter
cleek up, to hook or catch up
cloot, cloth
clootie cheese (see hingie)
clootie dumplin, a dumpling
wrapped in a cloth and boiled
clyack shafe, sheaf made from the
last stalks cut at harvest
clyack supper, end of harvest meal
cocker (aboot), to be unsteady
cockerty, rocky, unsteady
cog, frost-nail on horse-shoe
coggie, wooden container made of
staves, a pail or bowl
cog-hole, a hole for frost nails in a
horse-shoe
connach, to waste, spoil
coo-binnin, cattle binding
coort, a large open shed for
wintering cattle
corseckie, a kind of smock, worn
for dusty farm jobs
cowp, to tip, empty
crap o e waa, wall-head
creesh, grease, fat
creeshy, greasy, fat
crop, haircut
croshied, crotcheted
crudes, curds
cry in by, call at
cuffins, fragments of straw
cut, a length of yarn
cuttie, a short clay pipe
cweed, cud
cyack, 'cake', oatcake
dallie, doll
danner, stroll
dee, to do
deet, died

142

Glossary

deid-thraa, death throe
deil, 'devil', shoemakers' last
deny, refuse to move
dibber-dabber, to bargain
dicht, sweep, clean
ding, a showy person, show
dingy, showy
dinnle, of wheels, rumbling
dird, batter
dist, particles of meal and husks
    from grinding
div, to do
divaal, cessation
divot, lump, sod
docken, dock plant
dossie doon, toss down
dother, daughter
doup, bottom
dover, to doze off
dreel, drill
dubby, muddy
duds, clothes
dusty miller, type of primula
dwine, fail in health
Dyod, God
e, reduced form of the
eel, of cows, dry
Eel, Yule
eel-mairt, ox slaughtered and
    salted for Yule and the winter
een till't, one extra
een, one
eence, once
eese, use
eez, his
eident, busy
eir, reduced form of there
eizel, ember
em, reduced form of them
ess, ash

faa oot, to fall out, quarrel
faa, to fall
faar, where
fairlies, odds and ends
fan, fanner, winnowing machine
fang, whang, chunk
farden, farthing
farrach, drive, energy
farrer, farther
fashious, troublesome
Fastern's Een, Shrove Tuesday
fee-ed, engaged as a farm servant
feerich, agitated state
feert, afraid
feesh, fetched
fess, to fetch
fingerin, a kind of worsted
firlot, a quarter of a bow, _c._ 35lbs
fit, 'foot', shoemaker's last
fit, what
fite, white
fither, whether
fitiver, whatever
flachter spaad, turf spade
flannel broth, soup of milk and
    barley
flap, a lie-down for a doze
fleein, flying
fleetins, thick curds that form on
    the top of boiled whey
fleg, fright
fluggin, flagon
flype, to turn outside in
foggy bee, wild bee
foggy-larick, moss-covered bark of
    larch
foo, how
fool, dirty
foon, foundation
foorach, buttermilk

foorich, bustle, confusion

forbye, besides

forrit, forward

fraucht, a load

frost hole, a hole for frost nails in a horse-shoe

fun buss, whin bush

funs, whins

fur up, to earth up

fur, furrow

fye, whey

fye-brose, brose made with whey

fykie, troublesome

gaad, 'goad', wand

gait, gaitin, a sheaf set up by itself, or in a small group with the heads bound together

gale, gable

gamie, gamekeeper

gang, to go

gar, to make, force

geck-neckit, having a slightly twisted neck

geed, gave

gey, very

girnel, meal, storage box

glammach, an eager grasp

goosers, gooseberries,

gorblet, of an egg, containing an unfledged chick

gorblin, newly-hatched bird

goustie, ghastly

gowl, to scowl

graip, dung fork

gravat, scarf

greep, byre-drain

grieve, head workman on a farm,

gweed, good,

gyang, row,

gyte, to set up sheaves in gaits

haad, to hold

haaker, hawker

haase, throat

hack, to chop firewood

hackie, notch

hackstock, block, chopping block for firewood

haip, a trashy woman

haipie, trashy

Hairst Play, 'harvest' or summer holiday from school

hairst, harvest

hairy tatties, a dish of mashed potatoes and flaked, dried salt fish

hait, hot

haive, heave

haivless, shiftless

halla, hollow

han-barra, hand barrow, sack barrow

happer, hopper

heck, rack for hay or straw in a byre

heich, high

her leen, on her own

herrie, rob (of a bird's nest)

hidna heen, would not have had

hingie, a soft cheese, dried by being hung in a cloth

hingin lum, canopy chimney

hingles, in the, in a lazy mood

hinner end, in the, in the end, at last

hoast, cough

honey ale, fermented harvest drink made with honey and yeast

hooick, small stack

howp, to sip

hummlie, a hornless cattle animal

hurl, to drive, to have a lift in a wheeled vehicle

hyow, hoe, to hoe

idder, other

idleseat, idleness

ill-peyed, in a bad mood

ingin, onion

intilt, into it

kail brose, brose made with the juice of boiled kail

kebbock, a cheese

kelpie, a water demon

kemple, a horse-load of straw

ken, to know

kinlin, kindling

kirkyaird, churchyard

kirn, harvest home meal

kist, chest

kitchie, something served as an addition or relish to plain food

knocklesnorum, swivel for tethering sheep

knotty tams, a dish of boiled milk with meal cast in

korter, quarter (of oatcakes)

kye, cattle

laigh, low

lair, to become bogged down

lame, piece of broken crockery

larick, larch

leen, lone

lichtnin, lightning

lippie, measure for bruised oats for feeding horse

loo warm, lukewarm

loon, boy

loot, let, emitted

lowe, flame

lowp, to jump

lowpie for spang, with a leap and a bound

lowse, stop work

maamie, of broth, thick and smooth

maan, must

maiden feast, harvest home meal

mair a dae, more to do

mait, food

mart, market

meal-an-ale, harvest home celebration meal

meal-in, a dish of milk with a piece of hot oatcakes crumbled into it

mealy dumpling, a round pudding of meal, fat and seasoning, boiled or steamed

mealy jimmie, mealy pudding

mert, animal killed for salting

midden lachter, the site of a dunghill

midden, dunghill

minoarem, noisy crowd

mishanter, mishap

mither, mother

mixter, mixture

mochy, moist

mollach, to loiter about

moofae, mouthful

moss, peat bog

mowser, moustache

muckle, large

mull, mill

mullert, miller

murly tuck, dish of oatcakes crumbled into milk

myang, to be very eager

naiter girs, grass growing wild

near-begyaan, miserly

neen, none
neep, a 'turnip' watch, from its
    round shape,
neep-click, turnip hook
neeperin, neighbouring,
neep-hasher, turnip slicer
neep-shaaver, turnip sowing
    machine
neep-shed, turnip shed
neesht, neist, next
nott, needed
o, reduced form of of
oman, woman
oo, wool
or lang, before long
Orkney
orrals, odds and ends
overlay, brander over fire
ower, too
oxter pooch, armpit bread pocket
Pace, Easter
palin, fence
pap o' the haase, uvula
peesee, lapwing
pick black, pitch black
pike, frost-nail on horse-shoe
pint, point
pint, shoe lace
pirk, to toss
pitowerlie, brander over fire,
pizzers, pease-meal
plooer, ploughman
plot, to scald
plump-churn, plunge churn
pock, pyock, bag, sack
poo, to pull
pooch, pocket
pooer, puller
pottich, porridge
pottit heid, meat from the head of

a cow, shredded and eaten cold
    in a jelly made from the stock
preen, pin
pron, residue of oat husks and
    meal
puckle, quantity
quarterer, a tramp, given lodgings
    and temporary work
quile, ember
quine, girl
raip, rope
raivel, to tangle
ran-dan, on the, having a good or
    wild time
rantle tree, bar in chimney for
    hanging pots etc above the fire
ream, cream, to skim off cream
redd up, tidy up
redd, to clear
reed, red
reek, smoke
reest, to roost
restin pole, wooden pole attached
    to a cart shaft with a chain,
    lowered to give the horse a rest
    from the full weight of a loaded
    cart
riv, hens' run
rive, to tear, burst
roch, rough
rodden, rowan
rosit, resin
rositty eyn, 'resinous end',
    shoemakers' thread
roup, sale
row, to roll, trundle
ruck, ruckie, stack
rummle, rumble
saat, salt
saiddle, 'saddle', iron socket laid

146

across the knees to hold a
shoemaker's last

saps, a dish of pieces of bread
soaked or boiled in milk

scam, to scorch

scone, a round bannock on a
girdle, of wheat flour, and cut
into 4 triangular pieces

scraan, scraps, rubbish

scull, shallow container for
turnips, etc

scushle roon, to shuffle round

search, milk sieve

seck-barra, sack barrow

sell, cattle binding

shafe, sheaf

shank, the leg of a stocking

sheel, de-husk grain

sheen, shoes

sheil, to shovel

siccan, such

siccar-soles, a cautious or greedy
person

sids, 'seeds', particles of oat bran

siller, 'silver', money

sitty, sooty

size, chives

skeely, skilful

skep, a straw bee-hive

skink, a shin or knuckle of beef

skirlin, screeching

skirly, fried meal and onions

skraich, screech

skwallach, to shout

skweel, school

skylie, slate pencil

skyte, to slip; a bad state of affairs

slider, part of a cattle binding

slokit, slaked, quenched

slype, lazy, worthless person

smatchet, impudent child

smiler, a large shoulder rake

smoor, smother

smytlich, to hang about

snaa bree, melted snow

snaa ploo, snow plough

snaavy, snowy,

snap an rattle (see murly tuck)

sned, scythe handle

sock, ploughshare

sodger, soldier

soo, a rectangular stack of straw

soor dook, buttermilk

soorick, sorrel

souter, shoemaker

sowens, flummery, made from
sids

spang, vigorous stride

speen mait, soft or semi liquid
food eaten with a spoon

speen, spoon

speer, to ask

speldin, a haddock or whiting,
split and dried or smoked

spen, spean, to wean

spice, pepper

spleet new, split new

sprot, rush

spurtle, a stirring stick

squaar, square

staa, stall, floor of stall

stame mull, steam mill

steek, to grip, clench

steer, to stir

steiler, 'steelyard', weighing
machine

stirk, young cattle beast past the
stage of getting milk

stock, 'chap', 'bloke'

stook, shock of grain

stoorum, a mixture of meal, cinnamon and warmed milk

storm stooks, sheaves set up in fours, in windy weather

stot, young bullock

stovies, stoved potatoes

straacht, straight

strae, straw

strae rape, straw rope

straik, cylinder of wood for levelling grain during measuring; to level grain with a straik

straik, scythe-sharpening board

streek, of a plough, to put in action

striddler, a second forker on a big grain stack

strooshle, showing off, trashy woman

styoo, dust

styooie, dusty

styter, to stagger

suet clootie, piece of cloth containing a lump of suet, for greasing the hot girdle

swats, liquor made by soaking oat husks for sowens

sweel, to swill

swey, hinged iron ratchet for hanging pots etc above the fire

swype, to sweep, brush

swyte, to sweat

sye, to sieve

sye-er, milk sieve

syne, then

tailer, tool for taking the tails off turnips, see tapner

taings, 'tongs', hinged wire-tightener in fencing

tam thoom, 'tom thumb', nasturtium

tapner, tool for taking tops off turnips, see turnip

tattie chapper, potato masher

tattie, potato

ted, term of endearment (also sarcastic) for a child

teem, empty

teen, taken

teeth, 'tooth', fragment of a rainbow, a sign of bad or changing weather

teetie, a little look

teuchit, lapwing

thack, thatch

thole, to put up with, endure

thoom piece, oatcake buttered with thumb, as a snack

thraahyeuk, device for twisting rope

tig, sudden notion

timmer-teened, 'timber-tuned', tone deaf, in singing

tit, tuft, bunch

tool, towel

toon, farm-town

toondie, 'townkeeper', the one whose turn it was to look after the farm on Sunday

toosht, tooshtie, small amount

toozle, dangling bit

totum, spinning top

trackie-pot, teapot

traivel, to walk

trammle, thrammle, swivel in cattle binding

tramp-pick, a crowbar with a bracket for pressing with the foot

travis, stall partition in byre

troch, trough

trycle, treacle

trypie troliebugs, worthless, showy woman

tummlin tam, hay gatherer

tyaave, struggle

tyangs, tongs

tyne, lose

umman, woman

up-draacht, upwards draught

vrocht, worked

wallapie, lapwing

wallie, well

weather gaugh,-gall,-gaw, withergaa, atmospheric condition indicating the coming of bad weather

wechts, weighing machine

weer, wire

wey, weigh

wheek, to whack (down)

wheelin, coarse worsted yarn

wheety, stingy

wick, a wicked person, naughty child

wik-eyn, week end

win casen, 'wind cast', blown down

wincey, cloth with a woollen weft and a linen or cotton warp

winner, to wonder

winnister, winnowing machine

winnlin, straw bundle

winter, to get, to have all of the harvest taken in and stacked

wir, our

wirset, worsted

wisker, wisk, wusk, knitting needle holder

wither, weather

wun, dried

wye, to weigh

wyve, 'weave', to knit

yalla-yirlin, yalla-yitie, yaldie-yite, yellow hammer

yavel, broth

yavellers, second day's broth

yirlin, yellow hammer

yirnt milk, curds, junke

yoam, warm smell

yokin, start of a spell of work

Index